Raising Kids in a Digital World

A Parent's Guide to Balance Screen Time, Enhance Focus & Build Digital Literacy While Raising Tech-Savvy Kids Ages 6-12 Without Tech Addiction

Rachael Miller

Table of Contents

Introduction: From Screen Time Battles to Digital Balance **6**

The Modern Parent's Digital Dilemma 6

The Creator-to-Consumer Framework Introduction 8

What This Book Will and Won't Do 11

How to Use This Guide 13

Chapter 1: Understanding Your Child's Digital Brain: Why Kids Get 'Hooked' and How to Break the Cycle **17**

The Science of Digital Dopamine (Simplified for Parents) 18

Why 'Just Five More Minutes' Never Works 21

Age-Specific Digital Development (6-8 vs 9-12) 24

Breaking the Cycle Without Going Cold Turkey 27

Chapter 2: The Creator-to-Consumer Ratio: Building Purpose in Screen Time **32**

What Makes a Creator vs Consumer Activity 33

The 70/30 Rule for Balanced Digital Habits 36

App & Platform Guide (6-8 vs 9-12) 38

Tracking Progress Without Micromanaging 42

Chapter 3: Setting Boundaries That Actually Work: Beyond Time Limits **47**

Why Traditional Time Limits Fail 48
Activity-Based Boundaries vs Time-Based Rules 51
Natural Consequences That Teach 54
Collaborative Digital Contract Creation 57
Chapter 4: The Post-Screen Meltdown Map: Smooth Transitions Every Time **63**
Natural Stopping Points vs Arbitrary Clocks 64
Transition Activities That Actually Work 67
De-escalation Scripts for Meltdowns 69
Teaching Self-Regulation Skills 73
Chapter 5: Navigating School Technology: When Devices Come Home **78**
Separating School Tech from Recreation 79
Homework vs Entertainment Boundaries 82
Working with Teachers on Digital Policies 85
Creating Tech-Free Homework Zones 88
Chapter 6: Building a Distraction-Free Home Environment **93**
Designing Focus-Friendly Spaces 94
User-Friendly Tech Setup and Parental Controls 96
The Parent Mirror: Modeling Digital Behavior 99
Creating Natural Screen-Free Zones 102
Chapter 7: The Boredom Benefit: Why Less Entertainment Means More Creativity **106**
Why Boredom Is Brain Training 107

The Instant Entertainment Trap ... 109
Building Tolerance for Quiet Time ... 112
High-Value Offline Activities for Tweens ... 115
Chapter 8: Digital Literacy for the Real World: Teaching Critical Thinking ... 121
Teaching 'Real vs Fake' for Elementary Ages ... 122
Surviving the Algorithm: Understanding Platform Design ... 125
Simple Privacy Lessons That Stick ... 128
Digital Empathy and Online Kindness ... 131
Chapter 9: Handling Peer Pressure and Gaming Culture ... 136
When 'Everyone Else Has It' Conversations ... 137
Understanding Gaming Giants and Social Currency ... 140
Financial Digital Literacy and Microtransactions ... 143
Delaying Social Media: The Age 13 Conversation ... 146
Chapter 10: Troubleshooting Common Challenges: Quick Solutions for Tough Situations ... 152
The Sneaky Device Use Problem ... 153
Sibling Digital Conflicts ... 156
When Parents and Grandparents Disagree ... 159
Recovering from Setbacks and Mistakes ... 162
Conclusion ... 166
Sources ... 170

INTRODUCTION

From Screen Time Battles to Digital Balance

The Modern Parent's Digital Dilemma

The tablet hits the kitchen floor at 6:47 PM. Your seven-year-old is screaming because you said five more minutes, and those five minutes are up. Dinner is half-cooked. Your work email just pinged with something marked "urgent." And somewhere in the back of your mind, a voice whispers: *You're doing this wrong. A good parent would have figured this out by now.*

Here is the thing: you're not doing it wrong. You're doing something genuinely hard, something no previous generation of parents has had to do, with almost no dependable playbook to follow.

A lot of traditional parenting wisdom was built for a different world. "Go play outside" worked when the alternative was boredom. "No TV until homework is done" made sense when the television lived in one room and could not follow your child into bed. But the digital world your kids live in now was built, deliberately, to push back against boundaries. The old rules do not apply because the thing you're trying to manage has changed.

And yes, it really is a game, with enormous financial stakes. The apps your children use are built by teams of behavioral psychologists, UX designers, and data scientists whose main metric is engagement. Autoplay, push notifications, the "streak" your kid begs to maintain, none of it is accidental. Somewhere in a product meeting, someone argued that feature would keep eyes on screens longer. This is a billion-dollar attention economy, and your six-year-old's focus is part of what gets sold. That context matters. When your child cannot put the device down, it is usually not weak willpower or bad parenting. It is that a lot of smart people spent a lot of time making stopping feel miserable.

So what do you do with that? You could panic. You could confiscate every device and declare your home a screen-free zone. You could also spiral into guilt about every hour you've already allowed.

Or you could get strategic.

That shift, from guilt to strategy, changes everything. Think about it like this: you would not walk into a high-stakes negotiation without preparation, without understanding what the other side wants and how they operate. Parenting in a digital world calls for the same posture. First, you learn how the attention traps work. Then you build your own system, one that fits your family and holds up on a random Tuesday, not just in theory.

The guilt you carry about screen time is mostly wasted energy. Every parent reading this has handed a child a tablet to survive a conference call, a long car ride, or the last thirty minutes before bedtime. That is not a character flaw. That is life. The question worth asking is not "have I already messed up?" It is: "What do I do starting now?"

Starting now means replacing reactive battles with proactive structure. It means moving from anxious guessing to informed choices. It also means noticing that the window you're in, with children between six and twelve, is one of the strongest chances you'll get to shape their relationship with technology while you still have meaningful leverage.

This guide gives you the strategy. Let's build it.

The Creator-to-Consumer Framework Introduction

The instinct to pull the plug is strong. When you watch your nine-year-old zombie-scroll through YouTube Shorts for forty-five minutes, the conclusion feels obvious: take the device away. Problem solved.

Except removal creates its own problems. Children who grow up in screen-free households can arrive at middle school and high school digitally unprepared, socially out of step with peers, and caught off guard by the tech-heavy academic environments waiting for them. Classrooms use learning management systems. Friend groups coordinate through messaging apps. Research happens online. A child with zero digital experience is at a real disadvantage.

A better answer starts with a different question. Instead of asking "how much screen time?" ask "what kind of screen time?"

That is the foundation of the Creator-to-Consumer Framework, and you'll see it throughout the chapters that follow. The concept is simple: screen time spent consuming (watching videos, scrolling feeds, playing purely passive games) hits your child's brain differently than screen time spent creating (building a simple website, coding a game, editing a photo project, writing a story using a digital tool). Consumption puts the brain in receive mode. Creation pulls in problem-solving, planning, and executive function, the exact cognitive skills you want your child to practice.

Here is what this looks like in practice:

A six-year-old consuming: Watching a cartoon playlist on autoplay for an hour, getting progressively more glazed, and melting down when it stops.

A six-year-old creating: Using a drawing app to design characters for a story she is inventing, asking you how to save her work, and voluntarily putting the tablet down because she wants to act out the story with her stuffed animals.

A ten-year-old consuming: Playing an addictive mobile game designed around loot boxes and reward cycles, losing track of time, becoming irritable when interrupted.

A ten-year-old creating: Using Scratch to code a simple animation, troubleshooting why a sprite will not move the right direction, and excitedly showing you the finished product.

Same device. Same screen. Very different outcomes.

The goal is a healthy ratio between these two modes. You will not eliminate consumption entirely, and you should not try. Watching a movie together on Friday night is genuinely fun (my favorite kind of "screen time" is the kind where everyone is on the couch watching the same thing). Playing a game for thirty minutes is fine. The change happens when you get intentional about tilting the balance toward creative, purposeful use.

Timing matters, too. Between ages six and twelve, your child's brain is in a critical period for habit formation, self-regulation, and identity development. Patterns established during these years get practiced into place. A child who learns to use technology as a tool for making things often carries that orientation into adolescence, when the stakes around social media, gaming, and digital independence jump fast. You're not only managing today's screen time. You're shaping your child's default relationship with technology for the next decade.

You can think of this as a high-return parenting investment. The work you put in now pays off when your child is thirteen and staring down social media, fifteen and juggling online coursework, and eighteen and stepping into a world that demands digital fluency plus the ability to focus.

The framework is easy to understand and practical right away. Each chapter ahead gives you specific tools to put it into action.

What This Book Will and Won't Do

You won't find scare tactics here. No grim statistics about rising anxiety rates meant to make you feel worse than you already do. No "your child's brain is being destroyed" headlines recycled as chapter openings. Fear sells, but it does not help. Shame might push a panicked decision at ten o'clock on a Tuesday night, but it won't build the kind of steady, workable system your family actually needs.

What you will find is a toolkit.

Every chapter offers practical, tested strategies you can use the same day you read them. These are not ideas that sound good in a parenting seminar and then fall apart when your eight-year-old is crying because his Minecraft time is over. They are approaches built for real households where both parents work, where kids have homework on Chromebooks, where the family shares a Netflix account, and where "just say no" has never been a realistic long-term plan.

You'll get scripts: actual words you can use in the moment. When your daughter says, "everyone at school plays Roblox and I'm the only one who can't," you'll have a response ready that validates her feelings and still holds the boundary. When your son argues that his screen time is educational, you'll know how to steer the conversation so he learns to evaluate that claim for himself.

You'll also see examples tailored to two developmental brackets. A strategy that works for a six-year-old won't always land with a twelve-year-old. Throughout these pages, you'll find guidance adapted for ages 6 to 8 and ages 9 to 12, because what a second-grader needs from you is different from what a fifth-grader needs.

Here is a before-and-after to make this concrete:

Before (reactive approach): Your ten-year-old has been on the iPad for two hours. You suddenly realize how much time has passed, feel a wave of guilt, and announce that screen time is over immediately. He protests. You escalate.

He slams a door. You feel terrible. Tomorrow the same cycle repeats.

After (strategic approach): You've set up a pre-agreed schedule with clear transition rituals (covered in Chapter 5). Your son knows that when his timer goes off, he has a five-minute wind-down period to save his progress and choose his next offline activity from a list you built together. The transition is calm. Not perfect every time, but calm far more often than before.

That is the kind of change this guide is designed to create: incremental, realistic, and compounding over time.

That word "incremental" matters. Perfection is a trap. You will have days when your child watches too much TV because you're sick. You'll have weekends where the iPad becomes a babysitter because life is a lot. That is not failure. That is parenting. The mindset here is progress over perfection. Small, consistent improvements in your family's digital habits add up over weeks and months, and one good decision today beats a flawless plan you never actually use.

How to Use This Guide

You have two paths through this material, and both are valid.

The Quick-Start Approach: If your household is in crisis mode, if screen time battles are happening daily and you need relief now, go directly to Chapter 4 (Setting Boundaries That Actually Work) and Chapter 5 (The Post-Screen Meltdown Map). Those two chapters give you immediate, usable systems for the most common pain points. Once things settle, loop back to the beginning and work through the rest at your own pace.

The Deep-Dive Approach: If you have the bandwidth to build from the ground up, start here and move through each chapter in order. The material is designed to build. Chapter 2 gives you the brain science behind why kids react the way they do to screens. Chapter 3 expands the Creator-to-Consumer Framework with specific tools and ratios. Each chapter after that adds new strategies onto the foundation you've already built.

In every chapter, you'll find age-specific adaptations. When a strategy needs to shift for a younger child (ages 6 to 8) versus an older child (ages 9 to 12), those adjustments are called out clearly. A boundary-setting conversation with a first-grader relies on simpler language and more concrete visual cues. The same conversation with a sixth-grader can include reasoning, negotiation, and even collaborative rule-making. Both are covered.

Here is a sample of how this looks in practice:

Script for ages 6 to 8: "When the timer beeps, the tablet goes on the charging station. Then you get to pick: coloring, building, or playing outside. Which one sounds fun?"

Script for ages 9 to 12: "We agreed on forty-five minutes today. When the timer goes off, save your work and put the laptop on the shelf. If you want to talk about adjusting the schedule, we can do that at our Sunday family check-in."

Same principle. Different execution. Both effective.

Each chapter also ends with a clear set of action steps, so you never finish a section thinking, "Okay, but what do I actually do?" You'll always walk away with specific next moves.

One more thing: this guide is built for families where technology is already part of the home. You're not starting from zero, and you don't need to pretend you are. Whether your child currently has thirty minutes of screen time a day or three hours, the strategies ahead meet you there and move you forward, without the lectures.

Your Quick-Start Action Steps:

- Choose your path: Quick-Start (Chapters 4 and 5 first) or Deep-Dive (begin with Chapter 2 and read sequentially).
- Pick one screen time moment this week to observe without intervening. Notice what your child is doing on

the screen, how long they've been on, and what happens when they stop. Write it down.

- Have a brief, low-pressure conversation with your child about one thing they enjoy creating (drawing, building, storytelling) versus one thing they enjoy watching. Listen without correcting.
- Set a single, specific intention for what you want to change about your family's screen time habits in the next thirty days. Write it somewhere visible.
- Return to Chapter 2 when you're ready to understand the science behind your child's screen behavior, and everything you've observed will click into place.

CHAPTER 1

Understanding Your Child's Digital Brain: Why Kids Get 'Hooked' and How to Break the Cycle

Seven-year-old Maya was playing an educational math game on her tablet. Her mother, Priya, watched from the kitchen, feeling good about the choice. Then the timer went off. "Time to stop, sweetie." Maya didn't look up. "One more level." Priya gave her the extra level. Then came another. And another. Twenty minutes later, when Priya finally lifted the tablet from Maya's hands, the screaming started. Tears. Accusations. A thrown pillow. Over a math game.

Priya did everything "right." She chose quality content. She set a timer. She gave warnings. And still, the ending felt like defusing a small, furious bomb.

If that scene sounds familiar, you're dealing with something more powerful than bad behavior or weak willpower. You're up against your child's neurochemistry. Once you understand how it works, the strategies in the chapters ahead will make a lot more sense.

The Science of Digital Dopamine (Simplified for Parents)

Your child's brain runs on a chemical messaging system, and one of the key messengers is dopamine. Dopamine often gets labeled the "pleasure chemical," but that's only part of it. A big job dopamine does is anticipation. It rises when the brain expects a reward, and that rise is what keeps us seeking, clicking, swiping, and scrolling.

This is where screen design gets very intentional. The stickiest apps, games, and platforms lean on what's called a variable reward schedule, a concept B.F. Skinner described decades ago. It's also the same basic mechanism behind slot machines. Instead of giving the same payoff every time, the system mixes it up. Sometimes your child opens a loot box and gets something amazing. Sometimes it's junk. Sometimes they refresh a feed and see something hilarious. Sometimes it's dull. The unpredictability is the hook.

When rewards arrive on a predictable schedule, the brain adapts quickly and interest fades. When rewards are randomized, the brain stays on alert. Each tap, refresh, or new level carries the possibility of something great, and the dopamine system responds to that possibility, often more strongly than it responds to the reward itself.

For children between six and twelve, this system hits harder than it does for most adults. Kids in this age range tend to show higher reward sensitivity, especially when the stimulus is fast, bright, and constantly changing. At the same time, the part of the brain that helps them hit the brakes is still coming online. The prefrontal cortex, which supports impulse control, long-term decision-making, and self-regulation, is still developing through adolescence and into the twenties, as shown in Jay Giedd's long-running MRI work on brain maturation. Meanwhile, the reward circuitry is already humming. It's like handing a kid a car with a powerful engine and brakes that are still being installed.

That mismatch explains something every parent has seen: your child often cannot "just stop." When you ask them to put down a device mid-game, you're asking a developing prefrontal cortex to override a reward system that's fully activated. For a six-year-old, that's roughly like telling an adult to walk away from a slot machine while the reels are spinning. Possible, sure. Easy, not even close. (I've watched even mild-mannered kids flip in seconds when a parent pauses the game at the exact wrong moment.)

Product design makes it tougher. Autoplay lines up the next video before the current one ends. Notification badges are often red, a color our brains treat as urgent and hard to ignore. Progress bars creep up to ninety-five percent and practically dare you to finish. Loot boxes glow and shake before opening, stretching anticipation right before the payoff. None of this happens by accident. These are choices, often tested and refined by UX teams who know exactly what keeps people engaged.

Between six and eight, kids are especially vulnerable to reward cues you can see and hear: bright colors, celebration sounds, animated characters cheering them on. Their brains crave novelty, and digital environments serve it up in rapid bursts. Real life can't compete on speed. Building a block tower takes minutes of effort for a brief moment of satisfaction. A well-designed app can hand out dozens of tiny rewards per minute.

Between nine and twelve, the trigger often shifts. Social validation like likes, comments, streaks, and group-chat reactions becomes the bigger driver. The reward system, already trained by years of fast feedback, starts responding to social signals with the same intensity it once reserved for stars, points, and cheering sound effects.

Seeing this clearly doesn't make your child's screen attachment a moral failing. It makes it a predictable brain response to carefully engineered stimuli. When your child is glued to a screen, you're watching a brain do what it was built to do: seek rewards and avoid losing them. The strategies that actually help are the ones built around that reality, not the ones that assume a child can muscle through with willpower alone.

Why 'Just Five More Minutes' Never Works

"Just five more minutes" is the most common negotiation in the digital parenting playbook. Your child asks. You grant it, because five minutes sounds reasonable. Then five becomes ten. Ten becomes fifteen. By the time you enforce the real ending, the conflict is usually worse than it would have been if you'd held the original boundary.

There's a brain-based reason for this: time blindness. Developing brains track time differently than adult brains. The prefrontal cortex contributes to time perception, and because it's still maturing in kids ages six through twelve, they tend to estimate time less accurately, especially when they're absorbed. Fifteen minutes of gaming can genuinely feel like three minutes. They are often not lying when they say they "just started." Their internal clock is getting drowned out by the intensity of the experience.

Mihaly Csikszentmihalyi's work on flow helps explain what you're seeing. When challenge meets skill and feedback comes fast, people slide into deep focus and lose track of time. Adults do this too. If you've ever watched one episode and suddenly realized it's midnight, you've been there. The difference is that an adult brain is usually better at snapping out of it when prompted. A child's brain, caught in a reward loop, fights the interruption harder.

This is why the negotiation trap backfires. Each time you grant "five more minutes," two things happen at once. First, your child gets another round of variable rewards during the extension, which makes the eventual stopping point even harder. It's not just extra time; it's extra anticipation. Second, your child learns that the boundary is flexible. Next time, they'll push earlier and push harder, because pushing worked.

Consider how this plays out differently by age:

For a seven-year-old, "Five more minutes, please?" is often real distress. They're absorbed, the transition feels abrupt, and their emotional regulation tools are limited. When you say yes and then later enforce the real ending, you often get a meltdown because they've gone through two transitions instead of one, and each one is harder than the last.

For an eleven-year-old, "Five more minutes" is often strategic. They've learned that the boundary bends. The request may come with supporting arguments: "I'm almost at a save point," or "I'm in the middle of a match with my friends." The negotiation is more polished, but the dynamic is the same. Each extension teaches the brain that resistance pays. Over weeks and months, that expectation becomes the default every time screen time is about to end.

So what works instead? Here's a preview of the transition strategies you'll find in Chapter 5:

Anchor to events, not minutes. Instead of "five more minutes," try "when this episode ends" or "after you finish this level." Concrete endpoints are easier for kids to anticipate than abstract time units they don't feel accurately yet.

Use a two-warning runway. Give a ten-minute warning and a two-minute warning. The first warning gives the brain a chance to start disengaging. The second one makes it clear the ending is real and close.

Name the next activity specifically. "Time to stop" creates a vacuum. Your child's brain hears, "I'm taking away your reward with nothing to replace it." Try: "When this round ends, we're making tacos together." Now the brain has a new target to move toward.

A script that puts this together for a younger child: "Hey, Maya. Two more minutes, and then we're picking out your pajamas together. I'll let you choose the fuzzy ones or the dinosaur ones." You've named a short time frame, you have a clear next step, and you've added a small choice.

For an older child: "Jake, after this match wraps up, we're setting the table. You get to pick the music while we do it." The ending is tied to a natural stopping point, the next activity is specific, and there's a bit of autonomy built in.

These approaches work because they fit the brain's limits instead of pretending those limits aren't there. Chapter 5 gets into the details. For now, the core idea is simple: stop bargaining with the reward system and start setting endings your child can actually follow.

Age-Specific Digital Development (6-8 vs 9-12)

Lumping all children between six and twelve together when talking about screens is like saying teenagers and adults take the same risks for the same reasons. A six-year-old's digital brain and a twelve-year-old's digital brain are working with very different tools. A strategy that helps one age group can easily backfire with the other.

Impulse control milestones develop along a rough, fairly predictable timeline. Between six and eight, kids are just starting to practice basic impulse regulation. A six-year-old can follow a one-step instruction to stop an activity, but holding that line when the activity is highly stimulating takes enormous effort. Around eight, many children start to manage two-step self-regulation, like weighing what they want against what they've been told to do. It's still fragile and inconsistent, but it's there.

Between nine and twelve, impulse control becomes more reliable in low-stimulation settings. Kids in this range can delay gratification in class, wait their turn, and follow multistep instructions with growing consistency. A ten-year-old can usually stop reading a physical book when asked without drama. Put that same child in a high-reward digital environment, though, and you may see the same struggle you'd expect from a younger kid. Impulse control is context-dependent. The brain learns regulation in calm situations first, and only gradually transfers that skill to higher-stimulation moments. Digital environments are among the most stimulating contexts kids run into, so self-regulation often lags there compared to calmer settings.

That's why a nine-year-old who seems "old enough to manage screen time" can still fall apart when it's time to stop gaming. Their self-regulation is real. It's just not sturdy enough yet for this particular challenge.

Social pressure runs on different frequencies across these age groups. Between six and eight, social dynamics around screens are mostly logistical. "Can I play what my friend plays?" "Everyone at school talks about this show." The desire is about inclusion and shared experience, and it's often easier to redirect. You can offer alternative shared activities, or encourage your child to talk about what they're building or drawing instead of what they're watching, and the social sting fades fast.

Between nine and twelve, the situation changes. Social status and belonging can get tied to digital participation in more complicated ways. Multiplayer games create real-time obligations: "If I log off, my team loses." Group chats create hierarchies: being "in the loop" versus being left out can hurt. A twelve-year-old who can't talk about the latest trending clip may face subtle, real exclusion at school. This pressure isn't imaginary. For kids this age, peer belonging is a core developmental need, and digital platforms have threaded themselves into how that belonging happens. Brushing it off with "real friends don't care about that stuff" often shuts down the exact conversation you want your child to keep having with you.

Effective responses look different, too. For a seven-year-old saying, "But everyone watches it," a simple acknowledgment can be enough: "I hear you. That sounds frustrating. In our family, we choose shows together. Want to pick something from our list?" For an eleven-year-old who faces real social consequences from being offline, you usually need a deeper talk: "I get that your friends are all in that group chat. Let's figure out a schedule where you can be part of the conversations that matter to you, and we'll also set clear times when the phone goes away." You're taking their social reality seriously while still holding structure.

Cognitive processing changes between these age groups also shape how kids interact with content. Six-to-eight-year-olds take in digital content with limited filters. Messaging, advertising, and prompts land without being recognized for what they are. When a game says, "Come back tomorrow for your daily reward!" a seven-year-old may experience it as a real obligation. Their brain isn't yet good at spotting persuasion.

Nine-to-twelve-year-olds begin developing what psychologists call metacognition: the ability to think about their own thinking. It's a big cognitive shift, and it gives parents a practical opening. A ten-year-old can start to understand, with coaching, that an app is designed to keep them playing. "See how it shows you what you'll earn if you play one more round? That's not an accident. Someone built that to keep you going." That conversation is usually too abstract for most six-year-olds, but it can be genuinely useful for older kids. It also sets up the digital literacy skills covered in Chapter 9.

When you know where your child sits on these continuums, you can calibrate expectations. A six-year-old needs external boundaries with minimal explanation. An eight-year-old benefits from a simple reason behind the rule. A ten-year-old can help set boundaries collaboratively. A twelve-year-old often needs the "why" before they'll buy in. Same family, very different approach.

Breaking the Cycle Without Going Cold Turkey

When parents hit the "something has to change" moment, dramatic action can feel tempting. Take away all the devices. Cancel the subscriptions. Replace screens with board games and library trips. That impulse makes sense. When something feels out of control, a total reset sounds like the fastest way to get control back.

But sudden, sweeping changes to a child's digital routine usually create more problems than they solve. Here's why: your child's brain has built well-worn pathways around current screen habits. Those pathways get reinforced every time they grab the tablet after school, every time they hear the startup sound of a favorite game, every time they sit in the same spot on the couch to watch videos. These are not just habits. They're grooves built by repetition and reinforced by reward.

If you eliminate screens overnight, you remove the stimulus but you don't replace the pathways. The brain is left with the craving and none of the alternate routines needed to redirect it. When an expected reward disappears, the result is often agitation, irritability, and sometimes something that looks a lot like grief. A child who loses all screen access overnight may be harder to manage in the short term, not easier. And for many families, that hard week becomes the reason the plan gets abandoned: "We tried cutting back and it was a disaster, so we went back to how things were."

Gradual change works because it gives the brain time to adjust and build replacements. Each small tweak, shaving off fifteen minutes here, adding a post-screen routine there, nudges the system toward a new normal. The old pathways weaken with less use. New ones strengthen through repetition.

In practice, it can look like this. If your child currently uses screens for two hours after school, start by replacing the last twenty minutes with one specific alternative. Not "go find something to do," which leaves a vacuum the brain will fill with frustration. Pick something concrete: a cooking task, an art project already set out on the table, a walk to the park with the dog. After a week, when that twenty-minute routine feels normal, adjust again. Reduce screen time by another fifteen minutes and fill it with another specific activity.

Consider two families implementing change:

The Robinsons decided on a Sunday night that nine-year-old Elijah's gaming had gotten out of hand. Monday morning, the console was in the closet. By Monday afternoon, Elijah was furious, tearful, and convinced his parents hated him. By Wednesday, the parents were exhausted from constant conflict. By Friday, the console was back, and nothing had changed.

The Patels identified the same problem with their eight-year-old daughter, Anaya. They kept the tablet but shortened the after-school window by fifteen minutes and set up a watercolor station at the kitchen table. Anaya grumbled the first two days, then started painting. The following week, they shortened screen time by another ten minutes and added a "help cook dinner" routine. Within a month, Anaya's total screen time had dropped by forty-five minutes a day, and the transitions happened without tears.

Same goal. Different execution. The Patel approach worked because it gave Anaya's brain time to adjust and it offered real replacements, not just restrictions.

Over time, this process builds new pathways. Each time your child spends twenty minutes painting instead of watching videos, the reward system starts responding to the painting, weakly at first, then more reliably. Neuroscientists call this experience-dependent plasticity: the brain reorganizes itself around what gets repeated and what carries emotional weight. Physical activity, creative tasks, social play, and unstructured outdoor time can all produce dopamine through slower, more sustainable routes.

If your child's screen habits feel entrenched, the useful fact is this: patterns can shift, but they shift through repetition, not speeches. A twelve-year-old with years of heavy screen use is still building new connections every day. Start with one change you can actually hold, then stack the next one on top of it. Skip the overnight overhaul if you know you won't survive the week that follows.

Your Action Steps:

- Observe one screen session this week and identify the variable reward mechanics at play. Is it loot boxes? Autoplay? Social notifications? Naming the mechanism is a practical first step toward taking some of its power away.
- Replace "five more minutes" with a specific, event-based ending this week. Try "after this level" or "when this episode finishes," and pair it with a clearly named next activity.
- Identify where your child falls on the 6-8 versus 9-12 spectrum for impulse control, social pressure, and cognitive processing. Adjust your expectations and language accordingly.
- Choose one twenty-minute block of current screen time to replace with a specific alternative activity. Set it up in advance so the transition has a real destination.
- Commit to gradual change over the next two weeks rather than an overnight overhaul. Small, consistent adjustments tend to hold longer than dramatic resets.

CHAPTER 2

The Creator-to-Consumer Ratio: Building Purpose in Screen Time

Seven-year-old Maya spent most Saturday mornings watching toy unboxing videos. One after another, the clips rolled, and she sat cross-legged on the couch absorbing thirty minutes, then forty-five, then over an hour of content someone else had made about products someone else had bought. Her mother, Priya, did not love it. But Maya was quiet and content, and Saturday mornings were the one window Priya had to catch up on email. Then one weekend, Priya handed Maya a shoebox, some markers, and her tablet, propped open to a free stop-motion app. "Make your own unboxing video," Priya said. Maya spent the next hour arranging toys, drawing backgrounds, and filming frame by frame. She watched the final ten-second clip at least twenty times, grinning every single replay. The total screen time that morning was almost identical. What happened during it was completely different.

That gap, consuming digital content versus making something with digital tools, is the core idea in this chapter. Once you can spot it, you can reshape your child's screen time without necessarily reducing it.

What Makes an Activity Creator vs. Consumer

A simple way to sort any screen activity is to ask one question: is your child making decisions, or is the screen making decisions for your child? Consumer activities put the algorithm or the content producer in the driver's seat. Your child watches, scrolls, taps "next," and reacts. Creator activities put your child in charge. They decide what to build, how to arrange it, what comes next, and when it is finished.

This distinction matters because the two categories use different mental gears. Passive consumption leans heavily on the brain's reward loop. Content arrives, dopamine bumps up, then the next piece arrives. Creation, on the other hand, pulls in planning, sequencing, problem-solving, and self-checking. Your child has to decide what they want, figure out how to get there, try something, look at the result, then adjust. Those are the same executive function skills that show up in schoolwork, friendships, and, later, jobs.

This is where I see parents get stuck: the line between creating and consuming can blur. A child playing Minecraft in creative mode, designing a building from scratch, is operating much closer to the creator end. A child watching someone else play Minecraft on YouTube is firmly on the consumer end. A child following a step-by-step Minecraft tutorial lands somewhere in the middle. The label alone does not tell you enough. You have to look at what your child is actually doing with their hands, their attention, and their choices during that session.

A few practical markers help you sort activities quickly:

Creator signals: Your child is producing something that did not exist before. They are making choices about color, sequence, structure, or content. They can show you a finished result, even a rough one. They hit problems and have to work through them. They express opinions about their own work ("I want to change this part").

Consumer signals: The content keeps flowing without your child initiating it. Autoplay or algorithmic suggestions drive the session forward. Your child would struggle to describe what they watched or did ten minutes after stopping. There is no artifact, no saved project, no piece of work to revisit.

Some activities genuinely sit in the middle, and that is fine. An educational game that requires strategic thinking, like a math puzzle app, is more mentally active than watching cartoons, even if it does not produce a saved project. A child remixing music on GarageBand is creating, even if the loops were premade. Look for the overall pattern across the week, not a forensic classification of every screen minute.

One concern parents raise is, "Creative apps still feel like a lot of effort for me to set up." That is worth addressing directly. A lot of creator activities for kids in the six-to-twelve range require very little parent involvement after the first session. The setup might take ten or fifteen minutes. You download the app, sit together for the first project, and walk through the basics. After that, most kids can run independently, especially once they realize how good it feels to make something. The mess, the trial and error, and the slightly wonky first attempts are part of the point. They are evidence your child is learning, not just being entertained.

The real shift is how you judge a screen session's value. Instead of asking, "How long were they on?" start asking, "What did they do while they were on?" A forty-minute session where your child built a digital comic strip has a different cognitive return than a forty-minute scroll through short-form video clips. Both show up as forty minutes in a tracking app. Only one builds skills that carry over.

Think of it this way: if your child spent forty minutes with physical LEGOs, you probably would not stress about the time. You would see what they built and recognize the planning, spatial reasoning, and creativity involved. Digital creation can work the same way when the tools are right and the activity is truly open-ended. Your job is to stack the deck so more of your child's screen sessions land on the creator side of the line.

The 70/30 Rule for Balanced Digital Habits

Once you can tell creator activities from consumer activities, the next question is proportion. What is a reasonable target? The ratio that works well for most families in this age range is 70/30: roughly seventy percent of your child's recreational screen time spent on creator or cognitively active activities, and thirty percent on passive consumption.

Why not aim for 100 percent creation? Because it is neither realistic nor necessary. Kids deserve downtime. A nine-year-old who wants to watch a favorite show after finishing homework is doing normal relaxation, and there is nothing wrong with that. Leisure viewing is part of life for adults and kids. The goal is proportion, so passive watching does not dominate the whole screen diet while creative, skill-building time gets squeezed out.

The 70/30 split is a weekly average, not a daily mandate. Some days will look nothing like others, and that flexibility is what makes the ratio livable.

Consider a practical example. Ten-year-old Jaden has about ninety minutes of recreational screen time on school days and roughly two and a half hours on weekends. Across a full week, that adds up to about twelve and a half hours. Under the 70/30 rule, around eight hours and forty-five minutes should involve active or creative engagement, and around three hours and forty-five minutes can be pure leisure watching or casual browsing. On a Tuesday when Jaden has soccer practice and limited free time, he might spend his entire thirty-minute screen window watching a show. On Saturday morning, he might spend two hours building a coding project in Scratch. The weekly math still works, even though individual days vary widely.

That flexibility matters because rigid daily rules tend to collapse under real family life. A sick day, a rainy holiday, or a week when a parent is traveling for work: any of those can blow up a perfect daily ratio. A weekly average absorbs the disruption without turning every off day into a failure.

So how do you start if your child's current ratio is closer to 10/90?

Do not flip the numbers overnight. That creates the same resistance as any sudden screen time cut. Instead, introduce one creator activity per week and let your child get comfortable. If they are currently spending six hours a week on passive YouTube, swap one of those hours for a creator app or a guided digital project. The following week, swap another hour. Within a month or two, you can move much closer to the 70/30 zone without picking a fight.

A useful script for introducing this shift sounds like: "You can absolutely keep watching your shows. I also found this app where you can make your own animations. Want to try it for twenty minutes before your show today?" When creation is framed as an addition, not a punishment, the power struggle tends to fade. A lot of kids, once they feel the satisfaction of making something, start reaching for creator activities on their own.

One principle keeps this grounded: measure progress, not perfection. If your family was at 10/90 in January and you are at 50/50 by March, that is a major shift in how your child engages with screens. Holding out for a perfect 70/30 before you acknowledge the change misses what is actually happening. Watch the direction, not the decimals.

App & Platform Guide (6-8 vs 9-12)

The fastest way to move your child from passive consumption to creation is to put the right tool in front of them at the right developmental stage. A six-year-old handed a platform built for twelve-year-olds will get frustrated and quit. A twelve-year-old given a tool designed for kindergartners will get bored and write the whole idea off. Age-appropriate recommendations can be the difference between a creative habit that sticks and a one-time experiment that fizzles.

Ages 6 to 8: Building Confidence Through Play

Children in this range are still developing fine motor control, reading fluency, and comfort with multi-step processes. The best creator tools here are visual, intuitive, and forgiving. Ideally, kids can produce a satisfying result in a single session, even the first one.

ScratchJr (free, tablet) is a strong starting point for early coding. Children snap together colorful blocks to make characters move, speak, and interact. There is no typing required. A six-year-old can build a short animated story in fifteen to twenty minutes, and the sense of accomplishment shows up fast.

Stop Motion Studio (free version available, tablet or phone) turns any collection of toys, clay figures, or paper cutouts into a short animated film. Kids take one photo at a time, move the objects slightly, then take another. The result is a real animation they made from start to finish. This app pairs well with physical craft supplies, which means part of the project happens off-screen.

Drawing and painting apps like Tayasui Sketches or the built-in drawing tools on most tablets let younger children create digital art with finger painting, stamps, and color mixing. These are low-barrier, high-satisfaction tools that need almost no setup from you.

For this age group, passive YouTube watching is one of the most common screen habits to redirect. A concrete swap: if your child watches toy review videos, show them how to make their own review. They can line up three toys, record a short video on the tablet's camera, and narrate which one they like best and why. The production quality will be laughable by adult standards and deeply impressive to a seven-year-old. That pride matters more than polish.

Ages 9 to 12: Depth and Real-World Skills

Older children in this range are ready for tools with more complexity, longer project timelines, and genuine skill-building. They are also more socially aware, which means platforms with community features, moderated and safe ones, can add motivation.

Scratch (free, browser-based, MIT) is the full version of ScratchJr and one of the best introductions to programming logic available. Kids build games, animations, and interactive stories using drag-and-drop code blocks. The Scratch online community lets them share projects and remix other users' work, which adds a collaborative element. Moderation is active, and the platform is designed for this age group.

Canva for Education (free, browser or app) gives older kids access to graphic design tools they can use to make posters, presentations, social media mockups, and simple videos. A ten-year-old interested in animals could design an infographic about endangered species. A twelve-year-old who loves basketball could create a stats poster for their favorite team. Templates lower the barrier to entry while still leaving room for real creative decisions.

GarageBand (free on Apple devices) lets kids compose music using loops, virtual instruments, and recording tools. A nine-year-old can layer drum beats and piano lines to create a short track in twenty minutes. An eleven-year-old can record a podcast episode about a favorite topic. Both activities build audio literacy that carries into plenty of future skills.

Digital art platforms like Procreate (paid, iPad) or Krita (free, computer) give artistically inclined kids a canvas with layers, brushes, and professional-grade features. The learning curve is steeper, but kids who already like drawing often find these tools absorbing. Pairing digital art with physical sketchwork keeps the creative process balanced across mediums.

For kids in this age bracket who currently spend most of their screen time on gaming videos or social media browsing, a good bridge is to connect the existing interest to a creation tool. A child who watches Minecraft videos can learn to build Minecraft mods or design texture packs. A child who follows gaming streamers can try recording their own gameplay commentary. The interest stays the same. The relationship to the screen changes.

A quick note on safety: every platform recommended here either has no social features, has heavily moderated community spaces, or can be used in offline or private mode.

Always review an app's sharing and messaging settings before handing it to your child, and start with the most restricted configuration. You can loosen settings later as trust and maturity develop.

Tracking Progress Without Micromanaging

The fastest way to kill your child's enthusiasm for creative screen time is to hover over every session with a clipboard and a timer. If the shift from consumption to creation starts to feel like homework monitored by a strict teacher, your child will push back, and fairly so. The tracking methods that tend to work in real homes are simple, visual, and at least partly child-led.

A Weekly Visual Tracker

For the six-to-eight range, a paper chart on the fridge can be enough. Draw two columns: "I Made Something" and "I Watched Something." After each screen session, your child adds a sticker or a checkmark to the right column. At the end of the week, you look at the chart together. No grades. No lecture. You are just noticing the pattern. Most kids, when they see visual proof that their creative output is growing, feel a quiet pride that nudges them toward more making. The chart becomes a mirror, not a scoreboard.

For older kids, ages nine through twelve, a digital version may feel more natural. A shared note on a phone or tablet where they jot a one-line description of what they made ("coded a new Scratch game," "drew a dragon in Procreate," "edited a stop-motion clip") does the same job. Some families use a shared photo album where the child drops screenshots or photos of finished projects throughout the week. Over time, that archive turns into a portfolio. Kids who can see their skills improving across weeks and months are more likely to stick with the habit.

Child-Led Documentation

The strongest version of tracking is when your child owns the process. Instead of you asking "what did you make today?" after every session, teach them to save their work and keep a brief record themselves. A nine-year-old can learn to screenshot a finished Scratch project and drag it into a "My Creations" folder. A seven-year-old can draw a quick picture of what they made, even a stick-figure version, in a physical notebook.

Here's a conversation that introduces this idea naturally:

Parent: "You've been making some really cool stuff lately. Want to start keeping a collection of everything you create? Like an artist's portfolio."

Child: "What's a portfolio?"

Parent: "It's where artists and designers save all their best work so they can look back and see how they've improved. Professionals do it. You could do a kid version."

Most children respond well to this framing because it treats them as a creator with a body of work, someone whose output is worth saving. That identity shift matters more than any specific app or any single ratio.

Celebrating Creative Wins

When your child finishes a project, acknowledge it with real specificity. "That's great" works. "I noticed you figured out how to make the character jump in your Scratch game, and that part is tricky" lands better. Specific feedback tells your child you actually watched what they did, and it reinforces the problem-solving, not just the finished product.

Some families set a weekly "show and tell," maybe during Friday dinner or Sunday breakfast, where each child shares something they made that week. This can work especially well with siblings because it creates positive attention without turning it into a contest. One kid shows a stop-motion clip, another shows a digital drawing, and both get their moment.

Try not to judge quality or compare it to professional work. A six-year-old's first stop-motion film will be shaky, poorly lit, and three seconds long. Celebrate it anyway, because the skills inside that three seconds, patience, sequencing, spatial reasoning, and basic tech fluency, are real. Quality improves with repetition. What you are protecting early on is the desire to keep making.

One last note on measurement: if you are spending more energy tracking the ratio than your child spends doing the activities, the system has gotten too complicated. The 70/30 idea, the chart, and the portfolio folder are meant to be lightweight. Keep them that way. Five minutes a week is plenty.

Your Action Steps:

- Sort your child's current screen activities into "creator" and "consumer" categories this week. Use the signals from this chapter: Are they making decisions, or is the screen making decisions for them?
- Introduce one age-appropriate creator app from the guide above. Sit with your child for the first session to get them started, then step back and let them explore independently.
- Set up a simple tracking method: a fridge chart for younger kids or a shared digital folder for older ones. Let your child take ownership of recording what they create.
- Aim for a realistic starting ratio based on where your family is right now. If you're currently at 10/90, target 30/70 as a first milestone and build from there.

- Schedule a weekly five-minute "show and tell" where your child shares something they made. Respond with specific, genuine feedback about the process, not just the result.

CHAPTER 3

Setting Boundaries That Actually Work: Beyond Time Limits

Sarah set the timer for thirty minutes, announced, "Screen time starts now," and went back to the kitchen to start dinner. Twenty-eight minutes later, her nine-year-old was locked into a Minecraft build, placing the final blocks on a castle he'd spent the whole session designing. Then the timer went off. She called out, "Time's up!" He didn't move. She tried again, louder. He begged for two more minutes. She held the line because consistency matters, right? He slammed the tablet onto the couch, stomped to his room, and the next forty-five minutes were a mess of tears, door slams, and resentment that hung over the rest of the evening. The cruel irony is that the screen activity itself had been great. He'd been planning, problem-solving, and creating. The blowup had nothing to do with the screen and everything to do with how the boundary was built.

Most parents have lived some version of this scene. After enough repeats, many start to wonder whether the rules themselves are the problem. They're partly right. The idea of limits around technology is solid. Kids really do need guardrails. But the usual format, rigid countdown timers, arbitrary minute allotments, and one-size-fits-all restrictions, tends to create more friction than it solves. This chapter offers another way. You're not abandoning boundaries. You're redesigning them so they hold, with less conflict and more cooperation from your child.

Why Traditional Time Limits Fail

In households with kids ages six through twelve, the most common digital boundary is a straightforward time cap. Thirty minutes on weekdays. An hour on weekends. The number changes from family to family, but the structure is the same: the clock starts, the clock stops, and whatever the child is doing has to end right then. On paper, it's clean and enforceable. In real life, it runs into three predictable problems.

Problem one: the stopping point feels random from the child's perspective. Adults understand that thirty minutes is thirty minutes no matter what happens inside it. Kids, especially six- to ten-year-olds, experience time through the rhythm of the activity. A YouTube video has a clear ending. A game level has a completion point. A drawing has that moment when the child decides it's done. When a timer blares at minute thirty, it almost never matches one of those natural endpoints. You're asking a child to walk away mid-sentence, mid-level, or mid-thought. For an adult, the rough equivalent is someone shutting your laptop in the middle of an important email. You'd comply, but you'd feel yanked. And you'd bring that irritation with you into whatever came next.

Problem two is biology. Kids in this age range are still developing the brain systems that handle planning, time perception, and self-control. Psychologist Russell Barkley often describes this as a kind of "time blindness," and even in kids without ADHD, you can see milder versions of it all the time. When a child is absorbed in a screen activity, their sense of elapsed time shrinks. Twenty minutes can honestly feel like five. So the timer doesn't just annoy them, it surprises them. When they say, "Already? I just started!" they're often reporting their real experience, not trying to be manipulative. That gap between clock time and felt time can instantly register as unfair. And unfairness is one of the quickest triggers for a meltdown in this age group.

Problem three is structural, and it's the one parents feel in their gut: rigid time limits practically invite a power struggle. If the only tool you have is "Time's up, hand it over," then every screen session ends the same way, with a confrontation. You become the enforcer. Your child becomes the resistor. After weeks of this, the roles harden. Your child stops experiencing you as someone helping them manage their world and starts experiencing you as the person who always ruins the good part. Meanwhile, you start dreading screen time itself because you know how it ends. Some parents describe feeling a knot in their stomach as soon as they hit start on the timer, already bracing for the fight on the other side.

What makes this especially frustrating is that the power struggle can swallow the benefit the boundary was supposed to deliver. Time limits are usually meant to protect balance, so screens don't crowd out physical play, reading, family interaction, and sleep. Those goals make sense. But when every session ends in conflict, the emotional cost starts to outweigh the structural win. Parents either burn out and stop enforcing, which can lead to unchecked screen use, or they double down and escalate consequences, which tends to deepen resentment. Neither path gets you the calm, balanced relationship with tech you're aiming for.

There's another issue hiding in plain sight: flat time limits treat all screen activities as equal. Thirty minutes of passively watching someone else play a game on YouTube counts the same as thirty minutes coding something simple in Scratch. Thirty minutes of random short-form videos counts the same as thirty minutes researching volcanoes for a school project. If you worked through the creator-to-consumer ratio in the previous chapter, you can already feel the mismatch. A boundary system that can't tell the difference between high-value and low-value screen use is a blunt instrument when you need something more precise.

None of this means time is irrelevant. Knowing roughly how long your child has been on a device still matters, especially for sleep and basic movement. But when time is the main mechanism for starting and stopping, the problems stack up. The next sections give you options that work with your child's psychology instead of constantly running into it.

Activity-Based Boundaries vs. Time-Based Rules

If time-based rules create conflict because they cut activities off at awkward moments, the alternative is pretty straightforward: build boundaries around the activities themselves. Activity-based boundaries define screen sessions by what your child is doing and where that activity naturally pauses, not by how many minutes have passed.

Here's the difference. A time-based rule sounds like, "You have thirty minutes of tablet time." An activity-based rule sounds like, "You can play until you finish this level, then we'll save and stop." Or, "You can watch two episodes, and when the second one ends, the screen goes off." Or, "You can work on your animation project until you finish the scene you're on."

It's a small language shift, but it changes the psychology. Activity-based boundaries give your child a finish line they can see coming. They have time to adjust mentally. And because the stopping point matches a natural pause, you're not yanking their brain out of a flow state. They're stopping at a natural break, not getting cut off mid-thought.

For children ages six through eight, pause points need to be concrete and obvious. "End of this episode" works because the credits roll and the show clearly stops. "Finish your drawing and save it" can work too, as long as you define what "finished" means before they start. Game levels are often effective, but you may need to sit with your child once or twice to see how long a level takes in that particular game. Some take three minutes. Others take twenty. Knowing the difference helps you set expectations you can actually keep.

For children ages nine through twelve, you can get more nuanced. A nine-year-old building in a sandbox game can agree to stop "when you've finished the house you're working on." A twelve-year-old editing a video can agree to stop "once you've exported the current version." These are project-based endpoints, and they come with a side benefit: kids practice finishing a chunk of what they started, which transfers well beyond screens.

Here's a practical script for introducing this approach:

Parent: "We're going to try something different with screen time. Instead of me setting a timer, we're going to agree on what you're going to do before you start, and you'll stop when that activity reaches a good pausing spot. So before you pick up the tablet, tell me: what are you planning to do?"

Child: "I want to play my racing game."

Parent: "Great. How many races feels like a good session?"

Child: "Ten!"

Parent: "That's a lot. How about three races? That gives you a solid session, and then we'll transition to something else."

Child: "Five?"

Parent: "Let's do four. And when the fourth race finishes, you save and put the tablet on the charger. Deal?"

That negotiation takes about thirty seconds, and it does something important: your child has ownership of the stopping point. They helped set it. When race four ends, the boundary doesn't feel like a surprise attack from outside. It feels like an agreement they had a hand in.

You can find pause points even inside longer activities. Between episodes is a natural break. Between missions or chapters in a story-driven game is another. If they're browsing creative content for inspiration, a pause point might be "once you've saved three ideas to your folder." The key is to name the pause before the session begins, not to scramble for one when you're ready for the screen to go off.

A practical concern parents raise is, "What if the activity takes longer than I want?" That's where time can still help, just not as the main lever. Set a soft time window, say forty-five minutes, as an outer guardrail, and use the activity-based approach inside that window. I keep one old-school kitchen timer around, but I treat it as a reminder, not a cut-off. If your child's chosen activity can't reach a reasonable pause point within the window, that's useful information. It might be an activity better saved for weekends, or it may mean you need to define a smaller chunk as the session goal. Activity leads. Time backs you up.

Natural Consequences That Teach

Every boundary needs a plan for what happens when it gets crossed. This is where many families default to punitive consequences: "If you don't get off the tablet when your time is up, no screens tomorrow." Punitive consequences are built on making a child feel bad enough that they comply next time. Sometimes that works in the short term. Most of the time it doesn't teach self-regulation, and it often escalates the adversarial dynamic that was already causing trouble.

Natural consequences work differently. A natural consequence is a result that follows logically from the behavior, so the child can see the connection between what they did and what happened next. The classic offline example is simple: if a child refuses to wear a coat, they feel cold. You didn't impose that. The world did. Your job is to build a structure where digital boundaries have that same cause-and-effect clarity.

Here's what it looks like in a home. If the agreement was four races and your child plays six, the next day's consequence is a shorter session: "Yesterday we agreed on four and you played six, so today's session will be two to balance it out." The logic is easy to follow. They took more than agreed, so the total adjusts. No anger, no punishment, and no lecture. Just cause and effect.

Before/After Scenario:

Before (punitive): Ten-year-old Aiden doesn't stop his game when the session ends. Dad takes the tablet and says, "That's it. No screens for the rest of the week." Aiden is furious. By Wednesday he's resentful and sneaking screen time on Mom's phone when Dad isn't looking. The boundary has collapsed, and trust has eroded on both sides.

After (natural consequence): Aiden doesn't stop when his session ends. Dad says calmly, "You went fifteen minutes past our agreement. Tomorrow's session will be one race shorter to make up the difference. Let's reset and try again." Aiden is disappointed but not outraged. The consequence is proportional and connected. The next day, he watches the clock a little more carefully.

The difference between logical and punitive consequences usually comes down to three questions. First, is the consequence related to the behavior? Losing screen time because you didn't stop on time is related. Losing a playdate because you didn't stop on time is not. Second, is it proportional? Reducing tomorrow's session by fifteen minutes because today went fifteen minutes over is proportional. Losing a week of screens because of one overshoot is not. Third, can the child see the connection quickly? If you need a long speech to make the consequence make sense, the connection probably isn't strong enough.

For children ages six through eight, keep consequences immediate and simple. A good framework is, "If we go over today, we start shorter tomorrow." Keep the adjustment small: five or ten minutes, one fewer episode, or one fewer game round. Young kids lose the thread if the consequence is delayed or complicated.

For children ages nine through twelve, you can introduce the idea of a "balance reset." Older kids tend to respond to fairness language because their sense of equity is getting sharper. "We're resetting the balance because yesterday got out of alignment." You can also let them propose the adjustment: "You went over by about twenty minutes. What feels fair to balance it out tomorrow?" Often, kids this age suggest something stricter than you would have picked, because they want to prove they can be trusted.

Consistency matters a lot here, but consistency isn't the same as rigidity. Consistency means your child can predict what happens when a boundary gets crossed. Tuesday's overshoot gets the same type of response as Thursday's overshoot. That doesn't mean you can never make an exception. If your child is in the middle of an online project with a friend and asks for ten extra minutes to finish together, that's not just stalling. It can be social awareness and decent communication. Saying yes in that moment isn't "giving in." It's showing flexibility inside a structure, which is the skill you want them to learn.

One last principle: natural consequences should leave your child a clear path back to full privileges. If crossing a boundary leads to a permanent or vague loss, they stop trying. The message you're going for is, "We adjust, we reset, and we try again tomorrow."

Collaborative Digital Contract Creation

The boundaries that stick best are often the ones kids help build. That can feel backwards at first. Why invite the person who wants unlimited screen access into the rule-making? Because participation changes how a child relates to the rule. They understand it better, and they're less likely to treat it like an external force you're using against them. When resistance drops, daily battles drop too. And that gives you back energy for the parts of family life you actually care about.

A digital contract is a written agreement between you and your child that spells out expectations, freedoms, and consequences around technology use. The word "contract" is useful. It signals that this is mutual, that both sides have responsibilities, and that it matters enough to put in writing.

Start with a conversation, not a rollout. Pick a neutral time, not the aftermath of a screen fight, and frame it as something you're building together.

Script for ages six through eight:

Parent: "We're going to make a screen time plan together. I want to hear your ideas about what's fair, and I'll share mine, and we'll write it down so we both remember what we agreed on."

Child: "Can I have more tablet time?"

Parent: "That's exactly the kind of thing we'll talk about. Let's start with this: what are your favorite things to do on the tablet? And what do you think a good stopping point looks like?"

Script for ages nine through twelve:

Parent: "I want to update how we handle technology in our house, and I want your input. You're old enough to have a real say in this. Let's sit down this weekend and draft an agreement together. Think about what you'd want included."

Age-appropriate negotiation means adjusting how much decision-making power you share. A seven-year-old can choose between two options you've pre-selected: "Would you rather have your screen session before dinner or after dinner?" A twelve-year-old can propose terms and make a case for them: "I think I should get extra time on weekends because I have more free time and I'm working on a bigger project." Your job is to listen, take their input seriously, and hold firm on the non-negotiables, like no screens during meals, devices out of bedrooms at night, and clear content restrictions.

Here is a template you can adapt for your family:

Our Family Digital Agreement

What I can use: (List specific devices and apps/sites approved for the child's age)

When I can use it: (Specify which days and which windows, e.g., "After homework, before dinner on weekdays; morning or afternoon on weekends")

How sessions start: (Child states what they plan to do before picking up the device)

How sessions end: (Define the natural stopping point. E.g., "After two episodes," "When I finish my current level," "When I've completed my project step")

If I go over the agreed session: (State the natural consequence. E.g., "Tomorrow's session is shorter by the same amount")

Screen-free zones: (List places where devices aren't allowed. E.g., dinner table, bedrooms after 8 PM, car rides under 30 minutes)

We will review this agreement: (Set a date, ideally every four to six weeks, to revisit and adjust)

Child's signature: ______________

Parent's signature: ______________

The signatures might seem like a small detail, but kids, especially between eight and twelve, tend to take signing something seriously. It turns the agreement from a verbal instruction they can claim they forgot into a physical document they helped write.

Review dates matter. A contract that never changes gets stale and stops matching your child's maturity. A four- to six-week review cycle gives you a natural moment to expand freedoms as trust grows, adjust consequences that aren't working, and add new apps or activities as interests change. It also gives your child something to work toward. "If the next six weeks go smoothly, we can talk about adding that new game to the approved list" is often more motivating than another lecture.

Before/After Scenario:

Before: Mom announces new screen rules on Monday morning. The kids argue. One child says, "That's not fair, Jake's mom lets him play way more." The rules last about a week before everyone forgets or stops caring.

After: Mom sits down with both kids on Sunday afternoon. They spend twenty minutes discussing what's working and what isn't. The kids suggest ideas, some reasonable, some wildly ambitious. They negotiate. They write it down together. Both kids sign it and stick it on the fridge. When a disagreement comes up on Wednesday, Mom points to the fridge: "What does our agreement say?" The child checks, sighs, and complies. In that moment, the fridge has more authority than Mom's voice, and that's fine.

One final consideration: include your own commitments as a parent. If you expect your child to put screens away during dinner, commit to putting your phone away too. If you expect them to say what they're doing before they start, be willing to answer when they ask what you're doing on your phone. Kids spot hypocrisy fast, and nothing wrecks a digital contract quicker than a parent who plays by different rules. Including your side signals respect and models what you want to see.

Your Action Steps:

- Identify three natural stopping points in your child's most-used apps or games this week. Sit with them during one session and notice where pauses naturally occur.
- Replace your next "time's up" moment with an activity-based boundary. Before the session starts, agree on what the child will do and where they'll stop.
- The next time your child overshoots a boundary, use a logical, proportional consequence instead of a punitive one. Keep your tone neutral and frame it as a balance adjustment.
- Set aside twenty minutes this weekend to draft a digital contract with your child. Use the template above or create your own. Let them contribute at least two rules. Sign it together.
- Put the contract somewhere visible, such as a fridge, a bulletin board, or the back of a door, and set a calendar reminder to review it in six weeks.

CHAPTER 4

The Post-Screen Meltdown Map: Smooth Transitions Every Time

Saturday morning, 10:47 a.m. Your eight-year-old has been playing Minecraft for forty-five minutes, and the agreed-up-on stopping point is approaching. You walk over, put on your calmest voice, and say, "Five more minutes, okay?" Your child nods without looking up. Five minutes later, you return. "Time's up." What follows is a scene you know too well: the whining escalates, the controller gets gripped tighter, tears arrive, and suddenly your peaceful weekend morning has become a negotiation standoff with a person who barely reaches your shoulder. The problem here isn't your child's character. The problem is that the transition itself was set up to fail.

Ending screen time is one of the most emotionally charged moments in family life with kids ages six through twelve. The previous chapter covered how to set boundaries and build agreements. This chapter is about what happens in the seconds, minutes, and emotions that surround the moment a screen goes dark. Think of it as your operational playbook for the transition itself: how to structure the ending, what to do in the gap between screens and the next activity, how to respond when things go sideways, and how to gradually hand the controls over to your child so they learn to manage these transitions themselves.

Natural Stopping Points vs Arbitrary Clocks

Most parents rely on the clock as the authority for ending screen time. Set a timer for thirty minutes, and when it rings, the session is over. On paper, this makes perfect sense. In practice, it creates a recurring collision between the logic of time and the psychology of engagement. A timer doesn't know that your child is three minutes away from finishing a level, halfway through a YouTube tutorial on origami, or in the middle of an online game with two friends. When the alarm sounds at an arbitrary moment, your child experiences it as an interruption, and the brain's response to interruption is frustration. You're essentially asking your child to abandon an open loop, and open loops are exactly what the brain resists closing prematurely.

Natural stopping points work differently. They align the end of screen time with a moment that already feels like a conclusion inside the activity itself. In a game, that might be the end of a round, the completion of a level, or reaching a save point. For a video, it's the end of the current episode or clip. For a creative app, it's finishing and saving a project. The difference in emotional experience is significant. Instead of

"I was ripped away from something," your child feels "I finished something."

To use natural stopping points effectively, you need to know what your child is actually doing on their device. Sit with them for ten minutes during a session this week. Ask them to show you where the natural pauses happen. In Roblox, it might be when a round ends. On YouTube Kids, it might be between videos rather than mid-video. In a drawing app, it might be after exporting a creation. Once you've identified these moments together, you can build agreements around them: "You can play until you finish this match" or "Watch until the end of this episode, then we're done."

You might say: "When your character gets back to the village, that's our stopping spot." For older kids, ages nine through twelve, you can shift more ownership: "You tell me where a good stopping place will be before you start, and we'll agree on it together." This small shift in agency changes the dynamic from parent-imposed cutoff to mutually agreed conclusion.

Now, about the five-minute warning. It has become almost reflexive parenting advice, yet it frequently backfires. Why? Because a five-minute warning often functions as a five-minute anxiety countdown. The child hears "five minutes" and either panics, trying to cram more activity into the remaining time, or dismisses it entirely because five minutes feels both too abstract and too short. A more effective approach, supported by child behavior research, is a single concrete warning such as "one more turn" or "finish this level," rather than repeated time-based warnings. You're giving the same signal that the end is coming, but you're anchoring it to something concrete inside the child's experience rather than to a number on a clock.

Visual timers can still play a supporting role, especially for younger children who benefit from seeing time represented physically. Sand timers, countdown apps with color changes from green to yellow to red, or even a simple kitchen timer placed where the child can see it all provide a visual cue. The key is to pair the visual timer with a natural stopping point rather than using it as the sole authority. For example: "The timer shows about ten minutes left. That should be enough for one more round. When that round ends, we stop." You've combined the time awareness with an activity-based ending, and that combination is far more effective than either one alone.

One practical note: expect the first few attempts to feel clunky. Your child may push back on the idea of stopping at a natural point, especially if they're used to arguing for "just five more minutes" on an open-ended timer. Stay consistent. After two or three weeks of practice, families often report that with consistent practice, meltdown frequency can drop significantly within weeks because the child begins to internalize the rhythm of play-to-stopping-point rather than play-until-interrupted.

Transition Activities That Actually Work

Even with a perfect stopping point, the moment after the screen goes dark can feel disorienting for a child. Suddenly, the living room is quiet, and nothing is demanding their attention. That gap between screen-off and whatever comes next is where meltdowns most often ignite. The solution is a bridge activity, something that eases the nervous system from high stimulation to a calmer baseline without requiring the child to go from sixty to zero in an instant.

Physical movement is the most reliable bridge. When a child has been sitting still and staring at a screen, their body has stored up restless energy while their brain has been overstimulated. A brief burst of physical activity addresses both simultaneously. This doesn't need to be elaborate. Jumping jacks in the living room, a quick walk to the mailbox, bouncing a ball in the driveway, or even a two-minute dance to a favorite song all serve the purpose.

For younger children (ages six through eight), make the bridge activity playful and specific. "Let's do ten frog jumps to the kitchen" works better than "go play outside." You're giving them a defined, short-duration physical task that replaces the screen's specificity with a new, clear objective.

For older kids (ages nine through twelve), movement can be more self-directed: "Take five minutes to shoot hoops or walk the dog before we start homework." The goal is the same, but the delivery respects their growing need for autonomy.

Sensory regulation tools offer another effective bridge, particularly for children who are more prone to sensory overload. A cold glass of water, a crunchy snack like an apple or carrots, handling a textured stress ball, or even stepping outside to feel fresh air on their skin all provide the nervous system with new, grounding input. Think of it as giving the brain a different channel to tune into. One family found that handing their seven-year-old a cold orange to peel immediately after screen time became a reliable ritual. The temperature, the texture, the smell, and the fine motor task of peeling all worked together to pull his attention out of the screen world and into the physical one.

Conversation-based bridges work well too, but with a specific approach. Instead of asking "How was your game?" which often gets a one-word answer, try asking about something concrete inside the experience: "What did you build today?" or "What was the hardest part of that level?" You're helping them close the mental loop of the activity through language rather than leaving it hanging.

Here's a sample transition sequence you can adapt:

Screen time ends at the natural stopping point. Child saves or finishes. Parent offers a brief physical bridge: "Let's go fill up the bird feeder together" or "Race me to the front door and back." After two to five minutes of movement, offer a sensory anchor: a snack, a drink, or a tactile activity. Then introduce the next part of the day: homework, dinner prep, free play.

The entire sequence takes five to ten minutes, and it replaces what used to be a five-to-fifteen-minute meltdown. That's a strong return on a small investment of planning.

One pattern to avoid: offering another screen as the bridge. A true bridge moves the child into a different sensory mode entirely.

De-escalation Scripts for Meltdowns

Even with natural stopping points and bridge activities in place, meltdowns will still happen sometimes. A bad day at school, tiredness, hunger, or simply a particularly gripping game can push a child past their coping threshold. When that happens, your response in the first thirty seconds shapes whether the moment escalates or resolves.

The most important principle is validation before redirection. When a child is mid-meltdown, their emotional brain has taken the steering wheel. Logic, reasoning, and rule-reminders cannot reach them in that state. What can reach them is the feeling of being understood. Validation doesn't mean agreeing with the behavior. It means acknowledging the emotion underneath it.

Here's what this sounds like in practice:

Your seven-year-old is crying because screen time ended. Instead of "We had a deal, and the deal was two episodes," try: "You're really upset. You were having a great time, and stopping feels awful right now." Pause. Let the words land. Once the intensity drops, you can gently redirect: "I know it's hard. Let's go get a snack and you can tell me about what you were watching."

For older kids, ages nine through twelve, validation sounds slightly different because they need to feel respected, not babied: "I get it. Stopping in the middle of something you're into is frustrating. That makes sense." Then redirect: "The agreement was to stop after this match, and you did. Let's figure out what's next."

Calm voice technique matters enormously here. When a child escalates, the natural parental instinct is to match their volume or intensity. Resist that pull. Drop your voice slightly lower and slower than normal. This isn't about being artificially soothing or condescending. It's about using your own nervous system regulation as a model for theirs. Children's emotional states are heavily influenced by the emotional state of the adult in the room. A calm, steady voice signals safety, and safety is what allows the emotional brain to release its grip.

Public scenarios require a modified approach. If your child has a screen-related meltdown in a restaurant, a car, or at a family gathering, the added layer of social pressure can make you want to either give in quickly or clamp down harshly. Neither serves you well. In public, keep your script short and your voice low. Get physically close to your child, at their eye level if possible, and use a brief validation: "I see you're upset. We're going to handle this." Then, if feasible, move to a less stimulating spot: the car, a hallway, a quieter corner. Once you're away from the audience, use the same validation-then-redirect approach you would at home.

A before-and-after example: The Rodriguez family used to end screen time by announcing "Tablets off, now" from across the room. Their nine-year-old would argue, their six-year-old would cry, and the next twenty minutes were chaos. After shifting their approach, the parents started sitting near the kids as screen time wound down, acknowledged the stopping point together, and used a consistent phrase: "Screens are done. I know. What should we do next?" Within three weeks, the meltdown frequency dropped from daily to about twice a week, and the intensity of those remaining episodes was noticeably lower. The parents hadn't changed the rules. They had changed the transition.

A few phrases to keep in your back pocket for meltdown moments:

"You're upset, and that's okay. I'm right here."

"Stopping is the hard part. You did the fun part really well."

"I hear you. Let's take a breath together and figure out what comes next."

"This feels big right now. It won't feel this big in ten minutes."

And phrases to retire permanently:

"Stop crying, it's just a game." (Dismisses their emotional experience.)

"If you act like this, no screens tomorrow." (Escalates the conflict with a threat during a moment when the child can't process consequences.)

"I told you this would happen." (Shaming, and completely unhelpful in the moment.)

The goal of de-escalation is to get through the moment with your relationship intact and the boundary still standing. You can always debrief later, when everyone is calm, about what happened and what could go differently next time. The meltdown itself is not the teaching moment. The conversation afterward is.

Teaching Self-Regulation Skills

Everything covered so far in this chapter involves the parent managing the transition. That's appropriate and necessary, especially for younger children whose prefrontal cortex is still years away from full development. But the long-term goal is to gradually transfer transition management from you to your child. Self-regulation around screen time is a skill, and like any skill, it develops through practice, scaffolding, and incremental independence.

Building internal timers is the first step. Fifteen minutes and forty-five minutes can feel identical when they're absorbed in a game. You can strengthen their internal clock with simple practice exercises outside of screen time. During car rides, ask: "How long do you think we've been driving?" During cooking, try: "Tell me when you think three minutes have passed." These low-stakes moments build temporal awareness that eventually transfers to screen use. Over months, your child starts developing a felt sense of how long they've been on a device, which replaces total dependence on external timers.

Self-monitoring strategies give children tools to check in with themselves during screen time. One effective method is the "body check" prompt. Teach your child to pause periodically and ask themselves: Are my eyes tired? Is my body stiff? Am I still having fun, or am I just scrolling? You can introduce this as a family practice first. Set a gentle chime to go off every twenty minutes during screen time, and when it sounds, everyone in the room, including you with your phone, does a quick body check. For a six-year-old, you might simplify it: "When you hear the chime, wiggle your fingers and toes and take one big breath." For a ten-year-old, the prompt can be more reflective: "Check in with yourself. Still enjoying this, or just killing time?"

Over weeks of practice, the external chime becomes less necessary. The child begins to notice their own fatigue, restlessness, or boredom without being prompted. This is self-monitoring in action, and it's one of the most valuable executive function skills your child can develop during this age window.

This means creating opportunities for your child to choose to stop screen time on their own, before a timer, a parent, or an agreement forces them to. Start small. On a weekend, tell your child: "You can have screen time this afternoon. I'm not setting a timer today. See if you can notice when you've had enough and stop on your own." The first few times, they may push far past a reasonable duration. That's expected. Resist the urge to intervene immediately. Afterward, have a non-judgmental conversation: "How did that feel? Did you notice a point where it stopped being fun?" That awareness becomes the seed of voluntary stopping.

A nine-year-old named Priya tried this exercise on a Saturday. Her parents gave her open-ended tablet time with one instruction: "See if you can find your own stopping point." She used the tablet for about seventy minutes, then came to her mom and said, "I think I'm done. My eyes feel weird." Her mom resisted the urge to say "That was too long" and instead responded: "You noticed your body telling you something. That's a really useful skill." By the third weekend, Priya was managing the transitions within a range her parents felt comfortable with, and the power struggles had almost entirely disappeared.

For younger children, voluntary unplugging practice works best in shorter, more contained experiments. Give your six-year-old a twenty-minute window and say: "See if you can stop before I come get you." Even if they stop at nineteen minutes and fifty seconds, celebrate the act of self-directed stopping. The duration matters less than the muscle of choosing to stop.

A simple progression over time looks like this: At ages six and seven, the parent identifies the stopping point and manages the transition. At ages eight and nine, the child helps choose the stopping point and is coached through the transition. At ages ten through twelve, the child identifies their own stopping point, monitors their own engagement, and practices voluntary stopping with increasing frequency. You're still present, still observing, still ready to step in. But you're shifting from director to coach to consultant.

This gradual transfer of control is one of the most powerful gifts you can give your child before adolescence arrives. When they eventually have a phone in their pocket with no parental timer attached,

Your Action Steps:

- This week, sit with your child during one screen session and identify together where the natural stopping points occur in their favorite app or game. Agree to use one of those points as the ending marker for the next session.
- Choose one bridge activity to test after the next screen-off moment: a physical task (jumping jacks, a walk, shooting hoops) or a sensory anchor (a cold drink, a crunchy snack, time outside). Try it for five consecutive days and notice whether transition friction decreases.
- Practice one validation script the next time a meltdown begins. Start with "You're really upset. That makes sense." and pause for thirty seconds before redirecting.
- Introduce a "body check" chime during screen time this weekend. Set a gentle alarm for every twenty minutes

and have everyone in the household, adults included, pause and check in with their body.

- Within the next month, try one voluntary unplugging experiment on a low-pressure day. Give your child screen time without a set timer and ask them to find their own stopping point. Discuss how it went afterward without judgment.

CHAPTER 5

Navigating School Technology: When Devices Come Home

The Chromebook arrived in Marcus's backpack on a Tuesday afternoon. His school had issued one to every third grader, and within forty-eight hours, the device had migrated from the kitchen table to the couch, then to his bedroom, and finally to his bed at 9:30 p.m. on a school night. When his mother, Priya, walked in to say goodnight, Marcus was watching YouTube videos of someone playing Minecraft. "It's for school," he said, without looking up. Priya stood in the doorway, wiped out from a ten-hour workday, and realized she had a new problem. The device that was supposed to support her son's education had quietly become a pipeline to unlimited entertainment, and it carried the school's logo on it like a permission slip.

If this sounds familiar, you're running into one of the most common friction points in modern parenting. School-issued technology blurs the line between education and entertainment in a way personal devices usually do not. When your child's homework lives on the same machine that streams videos, runs browser games, and opens chat platforms, the boundaries you've built around recreational screen time can crumble fast. In this chapter, you'll get a practical game plan for managing school devices at home, drawing a hard line between homework and play, communicating clearly with teachers, and setting up spaces that make focus more likely than distraction.

Separating School Tech from Recreation

The first challenge with school-issued devices is that they often show up with no parent-facing instructions. The school configures them for educational access, but the filters are not always as strict as you would assume. Many school Chromebooks and iPads allow access to YouTube (because teachers use educational videos), Google searches (because research is part of the curriculum), and sometimes even app stores. From your child's point of view, this device carries institutional authority. It belongs to the school, so they assume the rules must be different from the ones governing the family tablet.

So start with a simple move: set a clear physical boundary for the device. Treat the school Chromebook the way you would treat a work laptop you bring home from the office. It has a purpose, a home base, and hours. It does not follow anyone to the dinner table or the bedroom.

The Landing Pad System: Designate one specific spot in your home where the school device lives when it's not actively being used for homework. This could be a shelf in the kitchen, a charging station in the family room, or a drawer in a shared space. The device arrives home, goes to its landing pad, and only leaves when your child sits down to complete an assignment. When the assignment is finished, it goes right back.

With kids ages 6 to 8, this works best when the landing pad is visible and never changes. A small basket on the kitchen counter labeled "School Tech" makes the routine concrete. You might say: "Your Chromebook lives here, just like your lunchbox lives on that hook. When you need it for homework, you bring it to the table. When you're done, it goes back."

Kids ages 9 to 12 may push back with "I need it for a project" at odd hours. The landing pad still applies, but add a quick check-in. Before the device leaves the pad, your child tells you what they're working on and how long they expect to need it. This is not about distrust. It's about building the habit of intentional device use, which matters even more once middle school hits.

App and Access Restrictions: Even if the school controls the device's primary configuration, you still have options. Many school-issued Chromebooks allow parents to set supervised browsing hours through Google Family Link or similar tools. Ask your school's IT department what parental controls are available and what will conflict with the school's setup. If the device allows YouTube access, ask whether they can switch the account to YouTube Restricted Mode, which filters out a lot of non-educational content.

Some practical restrictions worth requesting or implementing:

- Ask the school to disable the device's app store for home use if games are showing up on it.
- Set Wi-Fi schedules on your home router so the school device can only connect during designated homework hours.
- If the device has a guest browsing mode, disable it. Guest mode often bypasses school-installed filters.

Time-Based Educational Limits: Even legitimate homework on a screen needs boundaries. For a lot of kids, productivity starts slipping after about 30 to 40 minutes in the 6 to 8 range, and after about 45 to 60 minutes for ages 9 to 12. Build breaks into the routine before your child hits the wall. A timer on the kitchen counter usually works better than a timer on the device itself because the boundary stays external and visible (I'm partial to an old-school twist timer because you can hear it from another room).

Priya, the mother from our opening scenario, put all three layers in place: a landing pad on the kitchen shelf, router-based time limits, and a 40-minute homework timer. Within a week, Marcus stopped hauling the Chromebook around the house. It became what it was always supposed to be: a tool with a specific function and a specific place.

Homework vs Entertainment Boundaries

Even with physical boundaries in place, the tougher challenge shows up inside the homework session itself. Your child is sitting at the table, the Chromebook is open, and from across the room it looks like productive work. But between the math assignment and the reading comprehension exercise, there's a five-minute detour to a browser game, a ten-minute rabbit hole into a YouTube video about slime, and a chat window where a classmate is sending memes. The device is technically being used "for school." The work is technically getting done. Still, a 30-minute assignment stretches into 90 minutes, and focus splinters with every tab switch.

Verifying Actual Assignments: One of the simplest, most effective strategies is a pre-homework check-in. Before your child opens the device, ask them to tell you (or write down) exactly what they need to complete. Most schools use a learning management system like Google Classroom, Canvas, or Seesaw. Spend five minutes during the first week of school learning how to access your child's assignment dashboard. Once you have that, verifying what needs to be done takes seconds.

For ages 6 to 8, the check-in can be as simple as: "Let's look at your assignments together before you start. What did your teacher post for today?" You review the list, confirm what's on deck, and then your child begins. When they say, "I'm finished," you can quickly cross-check against the list.

With ages 9 to 12, you can hand them more ownership: "Write down your three assignments before you open the laptop. When you're done with all three, close the laptop and let me know." That small shift builds planning and self-monitoring instead of training them to react to whatever the screen throws at them next.

Preventing Homework Procrastination Through Games: Children do not usually sit down and decide to avoid homework. It's subtler than that. The assignment feels hard or boring, so the brain looks for relief. A browser game or quick video delivers an instant hit that the math worksheet cannot compete with. If you recognize that pattern, you're more likely to respond with structure instead of frustration.

One effective method is the "Work Block" system. Your child works on one assignment with full focus for a set period (15 minutes for younger children, 25 minutes for older ones), then takes a five-minute break away from the screen. During the break, they can get a snack, stretch, or talk to you. The break is real, but it's offline. This mirrors the Pomodoro technique used by adults and teaches your child that breaks are earned and intentional, not quietly stolen from work time.

A before-and-after example: Before the Work Block system, ten-year-old Aiden's homework routine looked like this. He'd open his Chromebook at 4:15, toggle between his reading assignment and a dinosaur game, half-finish his math by 5:00, get called to dinner, then claim he "still had homework" and need the device again until 7:30. After implementing Work Blocks, Aiden's mother set a kitchen timer for 25 minutes. He completed his reading assignment in the first block, took a break to play with the dog, then finished math in the second block. Total screen time for homework: 50 minutes instead of three hours. Same assignments. Radically different experience.

Parent Monitoring Strategies: You do not need to hover over your child's shoulder for every homework session, and hovering can raise anxiety and chip away at autonomy. Instead, aim for what you might call strategic proximity. Stay in the same room, doing your own work. Glance at the screen now and then. Ask a casual question about what they're working on. That communicates presence without turning the table into a checkpoint.

For school devices specifically, check the browsing history once a week. Be upfront about it. Tell your child: "I check your school laptop's history on Sundays, just like the school's IT department can. It's part of how we take care of school property." When it is framed as shared responsibility instead of punishment, it is less likely to turn into a power struggle.

Working with Teachers on Digital Policies

Some of the most effective changes you can make happen through conversation with teachers and school administrators. A lot of parents hesitate, worried they'll sound difficult or anti-technology. But most teachers are dealing with the same issues you are. They watch students drift off-task on devices all day, and plenty of them appreciate parents who want to line up home routines with classroom expectations.

Advocacy Scripts for Parents: Productive conversations start with tone. Frame your concerns as collaborative problem-solving, not a complaint. You're not attacking the school's technology choices. You're trying to get clear on expectations so home and school are not working against each other.

Here's a script for an initial email to your child's teacher:

"Hi [Teacher Name], I'm working on building consistent screen-time boundaries at home, and I'd love to understand how the school device fits into homework expectations.

Could you help me with a few questions? How much of the nightly homework requires screen use? Are there any assignments that could be completed on paper if we preferred? What controls do you recommend parents use on the school device at home? I appreciate the work you're doing with technology in the classroom and want to make sure we're supporting the same habits at home. Thank you."

This script does three things. It shows you're proactive and supportive. It asks specific questions the teacher can actually answer. And it leaves the door open for ongoing communication without putting anyone on the defensive.

Reasonable Accommodation Requests: If your child is especially sensitive to screen-based distractions, or if you notice that device-heavy homework is ramping up anxiety or cutting into sleep, it's reasonable to ask for alternatives. These do not need to be formal or tied to a diagnosis. Many teachers will offer paper options when they understand a family's preference.

Requests that tend to land well include asking for a printed version of reading assignments instead of on-screen PDFs, requesting that homework be posted earlier in the day so you can review it before your child opens the device, and asking whether test prep can happen with physical flashcards or workbooks instead of online platforms.

For ages 6 to 8, where screen-based homework is usually lighter, a simple request for paper alternatives often solves the problem entirely. For ages 9 to 12, where digital platforms are more baked into the curriculum, aim to cut the unnecessary screen time rather than trying to eliminate screens altogether. The goal is intentional use, where time on the device is serving a real purpose.

Home-School Communication: The most sustainable approach is keeping a light, steady communication channel with your child's teacher, not reaching out only when things go sideways. At the beginning of the school year or semester, send a brief note explaining your family's approach. Something like: "We limit recreational screen time at home and keep school devices in a central location. If there are ever assignments that require extended screen time, a heads-up would be really helpful so we can plan accordingly."

That small investment can pay off quickly. Teachers who know your baseline can flag things early, like a new platform being introduced or a project that will require extra device time at home. Instead of scrambling after the fact, you can plan ahead and keep expectations consistent.

Creating Tech-Free Homework Zones

The physical environment where your child does homework has a real impact on focus. Studies in attention and environmental psychology repeatedly find that simply having a digital device nearby can reduce performance, even when it is not in use. Your child's brain spends energy resisting the temptation of the screen, which leaves less capacity for the assignment itself. If you want a change that often makes homework feel easier without changing a single worksheet, start with the space.

Physical Space Setup: A strong homework zone has three basic traits. It sits in a shared area where casual supervision happens naturally. It has a clear surface with only what your child needs. And it keeps the school device contained to that spot during use.

A kitchen or dining table works well for most families. If your child has a desk in their room, be honest about whether that space supports focused work. Bedrooms come with strong associations with relaxing and playing, which can chip away at concentration. If a bedroom desk is the only option, angle it toward a wall instead of the bed, and keep the school device's charger at the desk so the device does not wander.

A few practical setup tips: Keep pencils, paper, erasers, and other analog supplies within arm's reach at the homework station. When your child needs a physical tool, they should not have to leave the workspace and risk getting pulled into something else. A small caddy or pencil cup at the table makes offline tools the easiest option, which reduces the impulse to "just look something up" on the device.

If your child is 6 to 8, sit with them during the first few weeks of any new homework routine. Your presence helps them connect the space with focused effort. Over time, you can gradually increase your distance, shifting from sitting beside them to working nearby in the same room.

For ages 9 to 12, bring them into the setup. Ask what helps them focus and what throws them off. Kids this age are getting better at noticing their own patterns, and having them evaluate their workspace strengthens that skill. You may be surprised how many older children choose to keep devices farther away once they feel the difference in how quickly they finish.

Alternative Research Methods: One of the most common reasons children reach for a school device during homework is research. "I need to look something up" becomes the ramp to distraction. Some assignments genuinely require internet research. Many do not, and you can sidestep the issue by giving your child better offline options.

Build a small reference shelf near the homework zone. A dictionary, a thesaurus, an age-appropriate atlas, and a few subject-specific references (a math facts chart, a periodic table poster, a timeline of historical events) cover a surprising number of those "I need to look it up" moments. For younger children, picture encyclopedias and illustrated science guides can make offline research feel interesting instead of like a punishment.

When online research is truly necessary, use a "research sprint" approach. Your child identifies exactly what they need to find, opens the device, searches for that specific information, writes the answer on paper, and closes the device. Keep the interaction short and purposeful. At the start, you can sit nearby during research sprints and help your child practice targeted searching instead of wandering clicks.

A conversation that models this approach: "What exactly do you need to find out?" "I need to know what year the Declaration of Independence was signed." "Great. Open the laptop, search for that one fact, write it in your notes, and close the laptop. I'll time you. Let's see if you can do it in under two minutes." Turning research into a focused, timed challenge turns the device into a precision tool instead of an invitation to browse.

Focus-Supporting Environments: Beyond the physical layout, pay attention to the sensory environment of the homework zone. Background noise from a television or a sibling's tablet adds cognitive clutter and makes focused work harder. During homework time, screens in the shared space should be off for everyone in the family. That keeps the message simple and consistent.

Some children focus better with soft background music (instrumental, without lyrics) or with ambient sound. A small speaker with classical music or nature sounds can help certain kids settle in. Try it for a week, then ask your child if it helped or if it was annoying. Their input matters here, because buy-in is half the battle.

Lighting matters too. Natural light from a window supports alertness and mood, while dim or harsh fluorescent lighting can add fatigue. If homework happens later in the day, a warm desk lamp aimed at the work surface creates a pool of light that pulls attention back to the page.

The Chen family's experience shows how these elements can work together. Their daughter Lily, age nine, was spending over two hours on homework each evening, frequently drifting between her Chromebook and conversations happening around the house. They made three changes: moved her homework station to the dining table with a clear surface and a supply caddy, turned off the living room TV during homework time, and placed a small lamp on the table to create a defined workspace. Within two weeks, Lily's homework time dropped to 50 minutes on average. Her teacher reported improved quality in her written assignments. Nothing about the assignments had changed. The environment had changed, and Lily's focus changed with it.

Your Action Steps:

- Set up a device landing pad this week: choose one spot where the school device always returns after homework.
- Schedule your home router to limit the school device's internet access to designated homework hours.
- Send an introductory email to your child's teacher using the advocacy script, asking about screen-based homework expectations and paper alternatives.
- Build a small analog reference shelf near the homework station with a dictionary, thesaurus, and subject-specific resources.
- Establish a household rule: all recreational screens are off during homework time for every family member, adults included.

CHAPTER 6

Building a Distraction-Free Home Environment

Marcus, a software engineer and father of two, stood in his living room one Saturday morning and counted the screens. Two tablets on the couch. A laptop open on the kitchen counter. His phone on the coffee table, face up, notifications pulsing. His daughter's Chromebook still on the dining table from Friday's homework. The family TV glowing with a paused cartoon. A smart speaker blinking its blue ring on the bookshelf. Seven screens, four family members, and every room tugging someone toward something digital.

"We didn't plan this," he told his wife. "It just happened."

That slow accumulation is how most households end up surrounded by digital noise. Nobody sets out to fill every surface with a glowing rectangle. Devices arrive one at a time, each one useful on its own, until the physical environment itself starts working against focus, creativity, and basic family conversation. This chapter is about reversing that drift on purpose, shaping your home so the space supports your family's goals instead of competing with them.

Designing Focus-Friendly Spaces

The way a home is set up sends constant cues about what to do next. A room with a tablet on the coffee table, a TV remote within reach, and a phone charging on the nearest surface sends one message: consume. A room with art supplies on an open shelf, a half-finished puzzle on a side table, and library books stacked in a reading nook sends another: make something, try something, get curious. Neither room needs a rule. The environment does the talking.

Start by picking the two or three places where your child spends the most unstructured time. For most families, that is the living room and the child's bedroom. Walk through each space and look at what is visible at your child's eye level. If the first things they see are screens and screen gear, you have accidentally built a consumption zone. The fix is simple: make offline options easier to see and easier to grab than the digital ones.

For children ages six to eight, that usually means drawing supplies, building blocks, simple board games, and picture books at grabbing height. If your child has to open a closet, dig through a bin, and hunt down pieces before they can start, that extra friction pushes them toward the tablet that is already charged and waiting. Aim to cut the steps between your child and the offline activity down to one or two. A small rolling cart with crayons, paper, stickers, and scissors parked next to the couch can reset the default in a room.

For children ages nine to twelve, the same idea holds, but the materials change. A shelf with middle-grade novels, a sketchpad, a deck of cards, a beginner electronics kit, or a journal within easy reach competes better with a screen than anything buried in a bedroom closet. One family reported that simply moving their eleven-year-old's Rubik's Cube collection from his bedroom shelf to the kitchen counter changed how he spent the twenty minutes before dinner each evening. He went from scrolling YouTube to solving puzzles, without a single reminder.

Comfort beats looks in these spots. A reading corner only works if it is genuinely pleasant to sit in. A beanbag, a floor cushion with a small lamp, or even a pile of throw pillows next to a low bookshelf creates a "sticky" place kids return to on their own. Notice where your child naturally gravitates when screens are off. If they sprawl on the living room rug, put a basket of books and activities right there. Meet them where they already are instead of expecting them to march across the house to a designated "creative zone."

Lighting matters more than most parents expect. Screens bring their own glow, so they work even in dim rooms that make reading or drawing feel like work. If your child's favorite hangout spot has weak natural light, add a warm lamp and suddenly analog activities feel easier. The Gómez family noticed their eight-year-old twins consistently chose tablets over coloring books in the late afternoon. The dining table where the art supplies lived sat in a shadowy corner once the sun moved past the windows. A clip-on desk lamp fixed it within days.

You do not need to redesign your whole house. Make two changes this week. First, move one offline activity to a visible, easy-to-reach spot in your most-used family room. Second, move one device out of that room's line of sight. Put the tablet in a drawer, stash the TV remote when you are not using it, or move the charging cable to another room. These small shifts are what economists Richard Thaler and Cass Sunstein call "choice architecture." You are not removing choices. You are changing which choices feel easiest.

User-Friendly Tech Setup and Parental Controls

The best parental control is the one you set up once and then mostly forget about. A lot of parents avoid network-level settings because they sound technical. But routers and family-safety tools have gotten much simpler. You do not need to be a network engineer to filter content, set access windows, and keep devices in their proper lanes.

Begin with your home router. Most routers made after 2018 come with a companion app that lets you manage settings from your phone. Log in to your router's admin panel or download its app and look for three features: scheduled access, device grouping, and content filtering. Scheduled access lets you set time windows when specific devices can connect to the internet. Device grouping lets you create a profile for your children's devices and apply rules to the whole group at once. Content filtering blocks categories of websites, like adult content, gambling, or social media, across every device in that group.

If your router's built-in tools feel thin, a DNS-based filtering service can be a strong, free alternative. Services like CleanBrowsing or OpenDNS Family Shield work by changing one router setting so all internet traffic runs through a family-friendly filter. Setup usually takes under ten minutes and comes down to changing two numbers in your router's DNS settings. Your internet provider's help pages, or a quick search for your router model plus "change DNS settings," will walk you through it.

If you want something more hands-on without digging into router menus, plug-and-play devices like Gryphon or Circle sit between your router and your home network and give you an app dashboard. You can pause the internet for specific devices with one tap, set daily time limits, and review usage reports. These devices typically cost around forty to one hundred dollars and let you skip most of the technical setup.

Here is a practical setup that works for most families with children ages six to twelve:

Set your children's devices to have internet access only during approved hours. For a school-age child, that might be 3:30 p.m. to 6:00 p.m. on weekdays and 9:00 a.m. to 12:00 p.m. on weekends. Outside those hours, the device can still be used offline for drawing apps, pre-downloaded audiobooks, or writing, but it cannot connect to the web.

Enable SafeSearch on Google and Restricted Mode on YouTube across the network, not just on individual devices. Network-level settings stick even if a child figures out how to toggle the device-level switch.

Create a guest network with no filtering for adult devices. This keeps your browsing and work needs separate from the children's restrictions, and it also cuts down on "Can I use your phone?" as a workaround.

A common worry is, "Are we being too controlling?" It helps to think of these settings the way you would think of a fence around a playground. The fence gives kids room to move freely inside a safe boundary. They do not spend their day staring at the fence. A ten-year-old does not need the technical details of DNS filtering, either. A plain explanation is enough:

"Our home network has a filter that keeps out websites that aren't right for kids. It's like a strainer that catches the stuff we don't want and lets the good stuff through."

For older children (ages nine to twelve) who are more likely to push back, bring them into the setup. Show them the dashboard. Explain that the filters protect the whole family, and that adults need help with distractions, too. When kids understand the reason behind the rules and see the system applied consistently, you will usually get less resistance.

Revisit your settings once a month. Kids' needs shift quickly. A nine-year-old starting a school research project on ancient civilizations might need temporary access to a wider range of sites. Build your system so adjustments take thirty seconds, not thirty minutes. The point is a network that runs quietly in the background, not one that becomes a daily fight.

The Parent Mirror: Modeling Digital Behavior

Your child is watching you. Every time you check your phone at the dinner table, scroll while they are trying to tell you something, or fall asleep with a screen in your hand, you teach a lesson that lands harder than any rule on the fridge. Children ages six to twelve are prime copycats. They learn more from what they see than what they are told.

This section asks you to do something uncomfortable: look at your own phone habits without flinching.

Try this for the next three days. Each time you pick up your phone, pause for one second and ask yourself whether you picked it up for a clear purpose or out of habit. Common Sense Media has reported that parents spend multiple hours a day on screens for personal use. What makes it sneaky is how often it happens in fragments: a quick check, a two-minute scroll, a notification glance that turns into a fifteen-minute detour. Your child does not see the fragments. They see a parent whose attention keeps splitting.

The Patel family tried this after their seven-year-old asked, "Mom, why do you always look at your phone when I'm talking?" His mother, Priya, tracked her pickups for a day and counted sixty-three. "Most of them were nothing," she said. "I wasn't even looking for anything specific. My hand just reached for it." That awareness alone changed her behavior. She started leaving her phone in a kitchen drawer during after-school hours and noticed her son's requests for screen time dropped over the following weeks. He was not only copying her. He was reacting to her availability. When she was fully present, he felt less need to fill the gap with a device.

Family device-free times give this shift some structure. Pick windows that matter for connection: meals, the first fifteen minutes after school, and the last thirty minutes before bed work for many households. During those windows, every device goes to a designated spot. Every device includes yours. When a child sees your phone sitting in the charging station during dinner, the rule feels shared. When they see you sneak a glance under the table, the rule feels fake, and you will be negotiating again tomorrow.

A script for introducing this to your family:

"I've been thinking about how much time all of us, me included, spend looking at screens. I want us to try something together. During dinner and for thirty minutes before bed, all our devices go in the charging station. Mine too. Let's see how it feels for a week."

For children ages six to eight, keep it simple: "This is our time together without interruptions." For children ages nine to twelve, you can be more direct: "I've noticed my phone distracts me from being present with you, and I want to change that. This helps me, too."

Leading by example goes beyond those set times. If you want to look something up mid-conversation, say it out loud: "I'm going to check something on my phone. Give me thirty seconds, then I'll put it away." That narration teaches your child that phone use can be intentional instead of automatic. The same goes for small choices: reading a physical magazine instead of scrolling the news, writing a grocery list on paper instead of grabbing your phone, sitting in a waiting room without immediately reaching for a screen. Over time, those moments add up to a template your child can copy.

The biggest shift comes when you stop treating your screen habits as separate from your parenting plan. Your digital behavior is the plan.

Creating Natural Screen-Free Zones

Some rooms and situations almost beg to be screen-free. If you name those zones and stick to them, you reduce the number of daily decisions everyone has to make.

Bedrooms should top the list. The American Academy of Pediatrics has long warned against screens in kids' bedrooms because they are linked to later bedtimes and less sleep. Blue light gets most of the headlines, but the bigger issue is behavioral. A device in the bedroom turns a rest space into an entertainment space. Your child's brain starts pairing bed with stimulation instead of sleep. Remove screens from your child's bedroom, including tablets, phones, handheld gaming devices, and TVs. For children ages six to eight, this is often an easy change because the habit of private screen time has not fully set in. For children ages nine to twelve, expect pushback if bedtime screens have been part of the routine.

A script for the transition:

"Starting this week, all devices charge in the kitchen overnight. Your bedroom is for sleeping, reading, and relaxing. If you want to listen to music at bedtime, we'll set up a small speaker that isn't connected to the internet."

The dedicated speaker solves a common objection from older children who use devices for music or sleep sounds. A simple Bluetooth speaker loaded with a pre-set playlist gives them the audio they want without the screen that keeps them wired.

Dining areas come next. Meals are one of the few daily moments when most families sit in the same place at the same time. Keeping that window screen-free tends to improve conversation and connection, and distracted eating is also associated with overeating and lower satisfaction. The rule is straightforward: no devices at the table for anyone, at any meal. If the TV is visible from the table, turn it off. If a phone buzzes in someone's pocket, it stays there.

Cars are trickier, especially with long commutes or road trips. "No screens in the car, ever" might fall apart on a three-hour drive to the grandparents' house. A tiered approach is more realistic. For trips under thirty minutes, keep the car screen-free. Use the time for conversation, an audiobook through the car speakers (I'm partial to audiobooks on drives because everyone gets the same story instead of disappearing into separate screens), or simply looking out the window. For longer trips, screens can come out after the first thirty minutes, with a break every hour. That way, the car does not become an automatic screen zone, but you still have a plan for the stretches that test everyone's patience.

A conversation starter for car time:

"Before we turn anything on, let's play a game. Each person picks something outside the window that starts with the letter A, then B, and so on. We'll see how far we get."

Charging stations tie these zones together. Pick one central location in your home, like a kitchen counter, a hallway shelf, or a living room side table, and make it the family charging station. Every device charges there overnight. Every device returns there when it is not in active, approved use. That single habit stops devices from wandering into bedrooms, bathrooms, and other places where they tend to cause trouble.

The Nguyen family put a power strip on the kitchen counter with a small basket beside it. Phones, tablets, and the school Chromebook lived there whenever they were not in use. Their twelve-year-old complained at first about not having her phone in her room. Two weeks later, she mentioned she was sleeping better and stopped bringing it up. The charging station had simply become normal.

One practical tip for families with multiple children: label each spot on the charging station. A strip of masking tape with each family member's name cuts down on "That's my charger" arguments and makes it clear the system applies to everyone, including the parents.

Screen-free zones work because they take willpower out of the equation. Instead of relying on a child (or an adult) to make a good decision in the moment, the room makes the decision. The device is not there. There is less to negotiate.

Your Action Steps:

- Choose one high-traffic room and rearrange it this week: move one offline activity to a visible, accessible spot and relocate one device out of sight.
- Log in to your router's app or admin panel and set up scheduled internet access for your children's devices, limiting connectivity to approved hours.
- Track your own phone pickups for one day. Count each one and note whether it was intentional or habitual.
- Designate your family charging station. Set it up today with a power strip, labels, and a clear "all devices here by bedtime" rule.
- Announce one screen-free zone (start with the dining table) at your next family meal and commit to it together, your phone included.

CHAPTER 7

The Boredom Benefit: Why Less Entertainment Means More Creativity

A nine-year-old named Marco sat at the kitchen table on a rainy Saturday, chin propped on his fists, staring at the wall. His mother had put all screens away for the morning. For the first twenty minutes, he asked four times if he could watch something. She said no each time and kept folding laundry. By minute thirty, he had pulled a roll of masking tape from the junk drawer and started laying lines across the kitchen floor. By minute forty-five, he had invented an elaborate game involving two tennis balls, a cooking pot, and a point system he was explaining to his younger sister in exhausting detail. His mother later described the scene as "the most creative I've seen him in months."

That rainy Saturday holds a lesson worth sitting with. The discomfort Marco felt in those first twenty minutes was useful. His brain, cut off from the usual supply of prepackaged entertainment, did what brains do when they are not being fed constant input: it started making its own. What looked like restlessness on the outside was, on the inside, a real neurological shift with measurable benefits.

Why Boredom Is Brain Training

When a child has nothing to do, the brain does not actually go idle. It shifts into a mode neuroscientists call the Default Mode Network, or DMN. This network lights up when a person is not focused on an external task, and it supports some of the most important cognitive work a developing mind can do: self-reflection, imagination, future planning, and the ability to spot connections between seemingly unrelated ideas. So the moments when your child looks like they are doing absolutely nothing may be some of the most mentally active moments of their day.

In a 2014 study at the University of Central Lancashire, researchers Sandi Mann and Rebekah Cadman found that people who sat through a short, boring task before a creative challenge came up with more ideas, and more original ones, than people who jumped straight in. Boredom worked like a cognitive warm-up. It nudged the brain toward wider, more associative thinking instead of grabbing the first decent answer and stopping there. For children between six and twelve, whose neural pathways are still being built and strengthened through repetition, this matters a lot. Each time a child hits boredom and then invents a solution, whether it is a game, a drawing, or a couch-cushion engineering project, they are practicing the mental moves behind creative problem-solving.

An analogy that tends to land with kids is the workout one. Muscles grow under strain. If you always carry things for a child, their arms stay weak. If you always provide entertainment, their creative muscles do not get much work. Boredom is resistance training for the imagination.

It also stretches beyond creativity into problem-solving and executive function. When a bored child decides what to do next, they practice a whole chain of higher-order skills: naming what they want, scanning what is available, weighing options, committing to a plan, and adjusting when that plan falls apart. That sequence is basically what adults call "project management" at work. A seven-year-old who decides to build a fort, gathers blankets, realizes the blankets keep sliding, and then figures out how to use clothespins as clamps has just moved through problem identification, resource gathering, troubleshooting, and iteration. No app walked her through it.

Then there is attention span. Boredom builds the ability to tolerate low-stimulation moments, and that tolerance is a prerequisite for deep focus. A child who can sit through twenty minutes of "nothing" without melting down is a child who can later push through a long math problem, a slow chapter in a novel, or a complicated conversation with a friend. Being able to stay engaged when things are not instantly exciting is a strong predictor of academic and social success in the tween years and beyond.

Of course, boredom feels awful. Children will tell you that loudly and repeatedly. The urge to fix that feeling by handing over a tablet is real, especially when you are trying to get dinner on the table or finish a work email. But every time boredom gets rescued immediately by a screen, the child learns a specific lesson: discomfort gets solved by external entertainment, not by internal resourcefulness. Do that often enough and it compounds. They get less practiced at generating their own engagement and more dependent on being entertained.

Here is the reframe that changes things for a lot of parents: boredom is not a problem to solve. It is a condition to allow. Your child's "I'm bored" is not an emergency. It is often the moment right before their brain finds something to do, if you give it enough runway.

The Instant Entertainment Trap

Modern children have access to something no previous generation had at this scale: entertainment in any quantity, at any moment, with almost no effort. A seven-year-old in 2010 who wanted to watch a cartoon had to wait until it aired, or find the right DVD. A seven-year-old today can open an app and pick from thousands of videos, each one selected to match what their brain finds most stimulating.

The gap between wanting entertainment and getting it has shrunk to almost nothing.

That speed matters because of how dopamine works in the developing brain. Dopamine, the neurochemical tied to motivation and reward anticipation, is heavily shaped by expectation. When a reward arrives quickly and reliably, the brain adjusts its baseline expectations upward. Over time, it takes more stimulation to create the same feeling of satisfaction. Neuroscientists call this tolerance, which is the same basic mechanism behind any habituation cycle. A child who watches fast-paced YouTube content for an hour a day starts to treat that tempo as normal. Slower experiences, like reading, drawing, or playing outside, can start to register as flat. They are not inherently boring. They just cannot compete with a reward system that has been trained on high-intensity digital input.

You see the result in everyday life: a ten-year-old who insists there is "nothing to do" while standing in a room full of art supplies, board games, sports equipment, and a backyard. Those options are not truly invisible, but they can feel irrelevant to a brain calibrated for screen-level stimulation. Parents sometimes label this as laziness or ingratitude. It is usually a mismatch. The child's reward system has learned to expect a certain intensity, and offline activities sit below that threshold at first.

Patience takes a hit, too. Digital entertainment delivers instant outcomes. Tap a screen and something happens. Offline life runs on delays. Building a model can take days. Learning a card trick takes practice. Growing a plant takes weeks. A child whose main entertainment is screens gets fewer reps tolerating the gap between effort and payoff. Eventually that shows up as frustration with anything that requires sustained effort: homework, musical instruments, long board games, or even conversations that do not go their way immediately.

Take the before-and-after experience of a family with an eleven-year-old named Priya. Before making changes, Priya spent roughly three hours a day on her tablet between gaming and videos. On weekends she resisted almost every offline suggestion. Her parents described her as "impossible to interest in anything real." After they gradually reduced her daily screen entertainment to about seventy-five minutes over four weeks, using the transition strategies from earlier chapters, something shifted. In week three, Priya spent forty-five minutes reorganizing her bookshelf by color. In week four, she asked her father to teach her how to cook scrambled eggs. Her parents said she still asked for screen time, but the intensity dropped, and the world that had seemed "boring" started holding her attention again.

What Priya's parents were seeing was her dopamine baseline slowly recalibrating. As the steady supply of high-intensity stimulation decreased, her brain adjusted its expectations. Activities that had felt dull a few weeks earlier began to feel worth doing again. This does not happen overnight, and it can get worse before it gets easier. The first week of reduced screen entertainment can be rough, full of complaints, pacing, and declarations that "this family is so boring." That is the withdrawal phase. It is also the price of admission.

Real-world enjoyment changes socially, too. Kids whose entertainment is mostly screen-based sometimes struggle with unstructured playdates, family outings, or vacations that do not involve devices. A park or museum can feel slow compared to a video game. A playdate requires negotiation, compromise, and tolerance of someone else's ideas, which is less immediately rewarding than a curated digital experience. When instant entertainment stops dominating, it does not just bring back play. It makes being with other people easier to enjoy.

Building Tolerance for Quiet Time

If boredom helps and constant entertainment backfires, the practical question becomes: how do you get a child who is used to nonstop input to tolerate quiet? You treat it like any other tolerance-building skill. Start small, stay consistent, then increase gradually.

Begin with what you might call "micro-doses" of unstructured time. For a child aged six to eight who is used to screens filling every gap, start with ten minutes of device-free, activity-free time. Tell them plainly what is happening and why. A script for this conversation might sound like: "We're going to have ten minutes of quiet time. No screens, no music. You can sit, look around, draw, think, or just hang out. You don't need to do anything specific. Your brain is going to feel restless at first, and that's fine." For older children, nine to twelve, you can be more direct about the science: "Your brain is used to constant input. We're training it to be comfortable without that. It's like building a muscle. The first few times feel weird, and then it gets easier."

The key word in both scripts is "training." Kids in this age range respond well to the idea that they are building a skill, especially when you frame it as respect rather than punishment. This is something you are doing with them, not something you are doing to them.

Expect resistance in the first week. A child might spend the entire ten minutes complaining, fidgeting, or dramatically sighing. That is still a win. The goal is not immediate calm. The goal is exposure. They are learning that boredom is survivable and that nothing breaks when the input stops for a few minutes. By the second or third week, extend quiet time to fifteen or twenty minutes. Many families eventually land on a daily quiet period of twenty to thirty minutes, often after school or before dinner, where every family member, including parents, puts devices away and sits with whatever comes up.

Mindfulness can speed this up, but it does not need to look like formal meditation. For younger children, six to eight, try a simple "noticing game." Sit together in a room and take turns naming something you can see, hear, or feel. "I hear the refrigerator humming." "I see a shadow on the wall." "I feel the chair under my legs." This shifts attention away from the absence of entertainment and toward what is already there. (If I had to pick one, this is the practice I see families stick with most easily because it feels like a game, not a lecture.)

For older children, nine to twelve, guided breathing can work well as an entry point. Start with three minutes. Breathe in for four counts, hold for four counts, breathe out for six counts. Many families do this together at the start of quiet time, and kids who initially roll their eyes sometimes end up saying it "makes my brain feel slower," which is exactly the point. The prefrontal cortex, responsible for focus and decision-making, works better in a calmer neurological state. You are not trying to turn your child into a monk. You are giving their frontal lobe better working conditions.

Comfort with silence is a skill that carries into adulthood. Adults who cannot tolerate quiet reach for their phones in every waiting room, every elevator, or every slow moment. A child who learns to sit through quiet now has an easier time with boredom later, too.

A few practical tips for making quiet time stick. First, anchor it to an existing routine. "After homework, before dinner" is easier to remember than a random time. Second, participate yourself. Children spot double standards instantly. If you are scrolling while they sit in silence, the lesson becomes: quiet time is a punishment for being young, not something the family values. Third, do not grade their performance. If they spend quiet time lying on the floor staring at the ceiling, that counts. The only rule is no screens and no asking for screens.

High-Value Offline Activities for Tweens

Once your child starts tolerating unstructured time, parents usually ask the next question right away: "What should they actually do?" The honest answer is that one of the best things they can do is figure that out themselves. Self-directed exploration is where a lot of the cognitive payoff lives. Still, you can set the stage by stocking the environment with options that have a real chance of competing with screens.

The offline activities that pull kids away from devices most reliably share three traits: autonomy, risk, and mastery. Autonomy means the child controls the process and the outcome. Risk means there is a real possibility of failure, frustration, or surprise. Mastery means the activity has a skill curve, where you get noticeably better with practice. Screens offer all three, which is why they are so sticky. The trick is finding offline versions that deliver the same psychological rewards.

For ages six to eight, consider autonomy-building projects like a small garden plot or a few pots they can manage themselves. Let them choose what to grow. Provide seeds, soil, and basic instructions, then step back. The timeline is long, the feedback is slow, and the payoff, like eating a tomato they grew, lands in a way a game trophy does not. Cooking is another strong option for this age group. Start with simple recipes where they measure, stir, and watch ingredients turn into something real. A seven-year-old who makes pancakes from scratch and serves them to the family gets a kind of competence that a screen cannot replicate. Building projects work well, too: simple woodworking kits, snap circuits, or big cardboard-box construction with tape.

For ages nine to twelve, the stakes can be higher and the projects more complex. This is the age range where many kids are ready for genuine skill-building, and where the mastery element starts to matter a lot. Here are several categories that consistently compete with screens:

Physical making. Model building, sewing, leather working kits, origami, and small electronics projects all offer tangible results and a visible skill curve. A ten-year-old who learns to solder a simple circuit board gets to hold a finished object they made with their hands. That kind of proof hits differently than a digital badge.

Outdoor exploration. Give a nine-year-old a field guide to local birds or insects and a pair of binoculars, and something often clicks. The collecting instinct that makes games so compelling transfers well to real-world identification. "I've spotted fourteen species" scratches the same itch as "I've reached level fourteen." Geocaching, orienteering, and nature journaling can hook the same part of the brain.

Performance skills. Magic tricks, juggling, card flourishes, and yo-yo tricks share a structure that mirrors the best games: attempt, fail, improve, master, show off. The social currency of being "the kid who can do a cool trick" is real at this age, and it can carry them through the frustrating early stage where everything feels hard.

Strategic games. Chess, Go, complex card games, and tabletop role-playing games use the same strategic thinking that draws kids to video games, but add face-to-face interaction and remove many of the stimulation accelerators built into digital design. A lot of families notice that once a child learns chess or gets into a tabletop campaign, it becomes their preferred social activity.

Entrepreneurial projects. For kids closer to twelve, small business ventures offer autonomy, risk, and mastery in abundance. A lemonade stand, a dog-walking service, a handmade jewelry shop, or a neighborhood car wash all require planning, execution, and real-world feedback. Even small earnings can feel like concrete proof that they can make things happen.

One principle matters when you introduce these activities: do not over-structure them. If your child starts a garden, let them make mistakes. If they build something and it falls apart, let them troubleshoot before you step in. Autonomy only works if the child actually has control. A parent who hovers, corrects, and micromanages an offline activity can create the same dependency as a screen that does all the thinking. Your job is to provide materials, help when asked, and then back off.

A father named Derek described the turning point with his eleven-year-old son, who had been spending most of his free time on a building game on his tablet. Derek bought a set of basic woodworking tools and some scrap lumber and told his son he could build whatever he wanted in the garage, with one rule: ask before using the saw. Over the first weekend, his son built a lopsided birdhouse. It was objectively terrible. But he was prouder of that birdhouse than of anything he had built in the game because it was real. It sat on a post in the backyard. Birds eventually used it. The digital buildings looked better. The wooden one counted.

That gap between impressive and meaningful is where this really lands. When you cut the constant stream of easy entertainment, you make room for your child to bump into their own interests. The projects they choose during unstructured time, and the ones they return to, tell you a lot about what is actually sticking.

Your Action Steps:

- Introduce a daily "quiet time" of ten minutes this week, with no screens and no structured activity, and participate alongside your child.
- Pick one autonomy-building offline activity from the ideas above and stock the materials in a visible, easy-to-reach spot in your home.
- Use this script when your child says "I'm bored": "That's okay. Your brain is figuring out what to do next. I'll check in with you in fifteen minutes."
- Reduce one block of passive screen entertainment per day and leave that time intentionally unscheduled.

- Track what your child gravitates toward during unstructured time over the next two weeks and note any emerging interests worth supporting.

CHAPTER 8

Digital Literacy for the Real World: Teaching Critical Thinking

A nine-year-old named Priya came home from school last spring and told her mother that sharks could fly. She had proof. Someone in her class had shown her a video during lunch, and the footage looked completely real: a great white shark soaring over a beach town, fins spread like wings, people running. Priya's mother asked where the video came from. Priya shrugged. "The internet." When her mother sat down and searched with her, they found the original clip in about forty seconds. It was a visual effects reel made by a college student practicing CGI. The "news headline" overlaid on the video had been added as a joke. Priya stared at the screen for a long time. "But it looked so real," she said.

It did look real. That is the problem, and it is why digital literacy now sits right next to reading literacy for kids growing up on screens. According to Common Sense Media, kids ages eight to twelve average hours a day on entertainment screen media, and that is before you count schoolwork. The question is not whether they will run into bad information. It is whether they have the thinking tools to sort it.

This chapter gives you practical ways to build those tools. We start with spotting fake content, move into how platforms are built to keep attention, cover basic privacy habits, and end with how to reduce misunderstandings and cruelty in digital spaces.

Teaching "Real vs. Fake" for Elementary Ages

Most parents start with a version of: "Don't believe everything you see online." It is true, and it is almost useless by itself. Kids between six and twelve need moves they can actually use, because "be skeptical" is too abstract for a second grader.

Begin with a simple check that works across ages: the "Who said it, and how do they know?" test. When your child sees a claim online, whether it is an animal fact, a scary headline, or a wild statistic on a YouTube thumbnail, teach them to ask two questions. First, who is making this claim? Second, what are they using as evidence?

Even a seven-year-old can learn to look for clues. A post that says, "Scientists discovered that eating candy makes you smarter," should trigger: which scientists? Where is the study? If the answer is nowhere, that is the answer.

For kids ages six to eight, keep it visual and physical. Print out two versions of a simple claim, one from a well-known source like National Geographic Kids and one from a random social media post with no author. Lay them side by side on the kitchen table. Ask your child which one they would trust more, and why. Then point out the differences: one has an author name, a publication, and a date. The other has a flashy image and no details. Five minutes of this teaches pattern recognition that sticks.

With kids ages nine to twelve, go a step deeper. Introduce reverse image search. Show your child how to right-click an image (or long-press on a tablet) and search for where else it appears online. When Priya's mother did this with the flying shark video, they found dozens of results debunking it. That one action, looking it up instead of just accepting it, changes the habit. Your child moves from passive viewer to active investigator. If you want the simplest option, Google Lens is usually the easiest tool to demo on a phone because it feels like a magic trick the first time kids try it.

Manipulated content deserves its own conversation. Deepfakes and generated images are no longer niche. Your child will see doctored photos, altered videos, and generated text that mimics real people. A practical way to address this with elementary-age kids is a game called "Spot the Weird." Pull up known examples of generated images (many educational sites collect them) and challenge your child to find what looks off. Look for hands with too many fingers, text in the background that does not spell real words, or shadows falling in different directions. Now skepticism becomes a skill, not just a warning.

You can teach source credibility in layers. For younger kids, keep it plain: people who study something for a long time usually know more about it than strangers online. A doctor knows more about health than a person making videos in their bedroom. A marine biologist knows more about sharks than a random post.

For older kids, add the next idea: even experts can be wrong, which is why we check more than one reliable source. If one site says something surprising and ten other trustworthy places say the opposite, that first site might be the outlier.

Here is a script for introducing this at dinner or during a car ride:

"You know how in school, your teacher asks you to show your work in math? The internet works the same way. When someone makes a big claim, you can ask: where is your work? If they cannot show it, that does not mean they are lying, but it means you should keep looking before you believe it."

The goal is not to make your child suspicious of everything. It is to make questioning automatic, the way they learn to look both ways before crossing a street. At first it feels awkward and slow. Later, it is just what they do.

Surviving the Algorithm: Understanding Platform Design

A ten-year-old opens YouTube and watches one video about Minecraft builds. The next fifteen recommendations are also Minecraft builds. Then Minecraft survival tips. Then Minecraft speedruns. Then a creator doing a "Minecraft challenge" that is really a thinly disguised ad. The child did not choose that path. The recommendation system did, and its job is to keep them watching.

Most kids in the six-to-twelve range have no idea this is happening. They assume the app is showing them what is "popular" or "best." They do not realize that YouTube, TikTok, Netflix, and plenty of kid-focused apps use feedback systems designed to predict what will hold attention and then serve more of it. Explaining that, clearly and without drama, is one of the most useful digital literacy lessons you can offer.

For younger children, ages six to eight, use an analogy they already get. "Imagine you went to an ice cream shop and every time you picked chocolate, the shop hid all the other flavors and only showed you chocolate. You might start to think chocolate is the only flavor that exists. That is what the app does. It watches what you click, and then it shows you more of the same thing, because it wants you to keep clicking."

With older kids, ages nine to twelve, be direct about the money. "These apps make money when you watch ads. The longer you stay, the more ads you see, and the more money the company makes. So they built a system that studies what keeps you watching and feeds you more of it. That system is called an algorithm, and it is very good at its job. It is not trying to help you. It is trying to keep you here."

This is also where personalization matters. Your child's feed is different from their friend's feed, and it is different from yours. The system builds a profile based on taps, pauses, rewatches, and what they skip. Kids usually find this fascinating and a little creepy once you spell it out, which is a useful reaction. Awareness is the first step toward resisting the pull.

The algorithm is only part of it. Platforms also use habit-forming design: auto-play that starts the next video before the current one ends, infinite scroll with no natural stopping point, notification badges that create urgency, and streaks that make stepping away feel like a loss. These choices are made because they increase time on the app. When you frame it that way, you are not demonizing technology. You are explaining what it was built to do.

Teaching resistance strategies means giving your child practical moves they can use in the moment. Here are three that work:

The "Why am I still watching?" check. Teach your child to pause every ten to fifteen minutes and ask: "Am I watching this because I chose to, or because it just started playing?" If they cannot remember choosing the current video, that is the system doing its job, and it is a good time to stop.

The manual search habit. Instead of letting recommendations steer the whole session, encourage your child to type what they actually want to watch or learn before they start. It shifts them from passenger to driver.

The "three and done" rule. Before a session starts, your child picks three specific videos or pieces of content they want to see. When those three are finished, the session ends. That creates a stopping point the platform removes on purpose.

A father named Marcus tried the ice cream analogy with his seven-year-old daughter, and a week later she came to him and said, "Dad, YouTube is hiding the flavors again." She had noticed that after watching two cat videos, the entire homepage was cats. That moment of recognition is worth more than any filter, because it lives inside your child's head and goes with them.

Simple Privacy Lessons That Stick

Ask most eight-year-olds if they know what personal information is, and they will nod confidently. Then ask if they have ever typed their real name into a game, told someone in a chat what school they go to, or shared their birthday to get a special reward in an app. The confident nod usually turns into a sheepish pause.

Privacy for elementary-age kids needs to be concrete and repeatable. Abstract warnings about "data" and "hackers" bounce off most children. Specific rules and vivid comparisons tend to stick.

Start with personal information boundaries by using a framework called the "Lock It" list. This is a short, memorable set of information your child should never share online without a parent present:

Full name. Home address. School name. Phone number. Birthday (including birth year). Passwords. Photos that show their location (school building, house number, street signs).

For kids six to eight, explain it like this: "There are some things that belong just to our family, like our address and your full name. Online, people can seem friendly and still be strangers. We keep our Lock It list private the same way we keep our house key private. You would not hand your house key to someone you just met at the park."

For kids nine to twelve, connect it to what they already do online. "Every time you sign up for a game or an app, it asks for information. Some of that is fine, like choosing a username. But if it asks for your real name, your school, your location, or your photo, stop and come get me. Companies collect this information and sometimes share it with other companies. Once it is out there, you cannot take it back."

Password security is the next layer, and it is one where kids often enjoy the challenge. Teach your child that a good password is like a secret code only they know. A simple method is three random words and a number. "PurpleFrog42Rain" is far stronger than "password123" or a pet's name. Make a game out of creating the weirdest combinations. Then set two iron rules: never share passwords with friends (even best friends), and never reuse the same password everywhere.

A mother named Deborah discovered that her eleven-year-old son had used the same password for his school account, his gaming account, and a random quiz app he found on social media. When the quiz app was compromised (as low-security apps often are), the exposed password opened the door to everything else. Deborah used the incident as a lesson rather than a punishment. They spent an evening creating unique passwords for each account and writing them in a physical notebook kept in a desk drawer. Her son, rattled by the experience, became the family's self-appointed "password security officer," reminding everyone to update credentials every few months.

"Stranger danger" online needs an update from the old playground version. Kids in this age range interact with strangers in multiplayer games, comment sections, chat features, and even educational platforms with community tools. The core message is simple: someone being friendly online does not make them a friend. A person in a game who gives you free items, compliments your skills, or asks to chat privately is still a stranger, no matter how many hours you have played together.

Give your child a clear action plan: "If someone you do not know in real life asks you personal questions, wants to talk privately outside the game, asks you to keep the conversation secret from your parents, or makes you uncomfortable in any way, close the chat and come tell me. You will never be in trouble for telling me."

For kids nine to twelve, add this layer: "Some people online pretend to be kids but are actually adults. They can be patient and good at seeming trustworthy. You protect yourself by keeping conversations where other people can see them and by never sharing your Lock It list, no matter how friendly someone seems."

These conversations do not need to be scary. Frame them as smart habits, the same way you teach a child to wear a seatbelt.

Digital Empathy and Online Kindness

A twelve-year-old named Kai sent a text to his friend that said, "Nice job today." He meant it sincerely. His friend had scored the winning goal in their soccer game. But the friend read it as sarcasm, because an older kid at school had been using "nice job" sarcastically all week. The friend fired back an angry response. Kai was confused. Within an hour, three other kids had been pulled into the argument, sides had been chosen, and a group chat that had been friendly that morning was a mess by bedtime.

This kind of misunderstanding is common in digital communication because text strips away the cues we rely on to interpret meaning. There is no facial expression, no tone of voice, and no body language. A period at the end of a sentence can feel aggressive to a child who is used to texts without punctuation. Capital letters feel like shouting. A delayed response can feel like rejection. Adults misread this stuff, too. Kids, who are still learning social nuance, get tripped up even faster.

Teach your child the "Read It Twice" rule for tone misunderstandings. Before reacting to a message that feels mean or weird, read it again and imagine the person saying it with a smile. If it could be friendly, treat it like it is. If it still feels wrong after the second read, ask what they meant instead of assuming the worst. Give your child this script: "Hey, I was not sure what you meant by that. Were you joking?" That one question can stop a conflict before it gathers an audience.

For kids six to eight, keep the lesson simple: "Words on a screen do not have a voice. Sometimes what someone types sounds meaner than they meant it. If a message makes you feel bad, show me before you reply."

For kids nine to twelve, explore the nuance further. Talk about how emojis, punctuation, and even response speed change the way messages land. A thumbs-up emoji after a long, heartfelt message can feel dismissive. "K" instead of "okay" can feel cold. These are real social dynamics your child is trying to read without a manual.

Cyberbullying prevention starts with a clear definition. Bullying is repeated, intentional behavior designed to hurt someone. Online, it often looks like posting embarrassing photos or screenshots, excluding someone from group chats on purpose, spreading rumors, creating fake accounts to mock someone, or sending threatening or cruel messages. Your child needs to know what it looks like, what to do if it happens to them, and what to do if they see it happening to someone else.

If your child is the target: save evidence (screenshots), do not respond to the bully, block the person, and tell a trusted adult immediately. Make it clear that reporting is not tattling. "If someone was pushing you on the playground every day, you would tell me. This is the same thing, just in a different place."

If your child witnesses cyberbullying: do not join in, do not forward or share the content, support the person being targeted (even a private message saying "that was not okay, are you alright?" can matter a lot), and report it. Bystanders who step in can change the whole dynamic. A meta-analysis by Polanin, Espelage, and Pigott (2012) found that bullying prevention programs that train bystanders and peer responses can reduce bullying and victimization, which matches what many schools see on the ground.

If your child is the one doing it: this is the conversation no parent wants, but it comes up. Kids sometimes join pile-ons without fully grasping the impact. They forward a "funny" screenshot without thinking about the person in it. They send a mean message because their friends are doing it. Address the behavior directly: "What you did caused real pain to a real person. How would you feel if that message was about you?" Then focus on making it right, whether that means apologizing, deleting content, or losing device privileges for a period.

Online kindness is not mysterious. It is the same basic behavior you expect face to face, with one extra problem: the screen makes it easier to forget there is a person on the other side. Say that part out loud. "The person reading that has feelings exactly like yours. They have bad days. They get embarrassed. They want to be liked. Write like they are sitting next to you."

One family created a simple ritual: before their ten-year-old posted anything online or sent any message, she asked herself three questions. "Is it true? Is it kind? Would I say it to their face?" She did not always remember. But over time, the pause became more natural, and the quality of her online interactions improved noticeably.

This is not about raising a kid who is "nice" online. It is about lowering the odds that your child gets dragged into avoidable conflict and teaching them how to handle the messy moments when they do.

Your Action Steps:

- Introduce the "Who said it, and how do they know?" test this week using a real example from your child's recent screen time. Practice it together at least three times until the questions become familiar.

- Explain the algorithm to your child using the ice cream shop analogy (ages six to eight) or the business model explanation (ages nine to twelve), and implement the "three and done" rule for their next viewing session.
- Create a "Lock It" list with your child and post it near the family computer or device charging station. Review password security and update any reused or weak passwords together.
- Teach the "Read It Twice" rule and the script "Hey, I was not sure what you meant by that. Were you joking?" as the default response when a message feels hurtful or confusing.
- Have a direct conversation about cyberbullying this week: what it looks like, what to do as a target, as a bystander, and as a participant. Make sure your child knows they can always come to you without fear of losing their device as punishment for reporting.

CHAPTER 9

Handling Peer Pressure and Gaming Culture

The first time it happened, Marcus was driving his eight-year-old home from a birthday party. From the backseat came a voice that was equal parts frustration and accusation: "Dad, literally everyone in my class plays Fortnite. Everyone. I'm the only one who doesn't, and they all talk about it at lunch and I just have to sit there." Marcus gripped the steering wheel a little tighter. He could hear the real hurt in his son's voice. He also knew that "literally everyone" probably meant four or five kids. But in that moment, logic was beside the point. His child felt left out, and that feeling was completely real. Marcus had navigated boardroom negotiations, managed cross-functional teams, and delivered quarterly results under pressure. Yet this single backseat conversation felt more high-stakes than any of it.

If you have a child between six and twelve, some version of this conversation is coming. Maybe it already has. The details change with the year and the age group, but the pressure stays the same: your child feels like the odd one out because of a technology boundary you set, and they want you to fix it by removing that boundary. How you respond shapes more than a single screen-time decision. It teaches your child what to do with social pressure, how to weigh their own values against the crowd, and how to stay steady when everyone else seems to be moving in a direction that does not work for them.

When "Everyone Else Has It" Conversations

The "everyone else" argument lands because it taps a real developmental need. Kids between six and twelve are building their social identity, and belonging matters in a way that is hard to overstate. Brushing it off with a quick "I don't care what everyone else does" often backfires. Your child hears, "Your feelings don't matter," or, "Your social life is unimportant to me." Neither message builds the trust you will need later, when the decisions get bigger and the stakes go up in adolescence.

A better approach starts with validation, then redirection. Here is what that can sound like in practice:

For ages six to eight: "It sounds like you felt left out when the other kids were talking about that game. That is a really uncomfortable feeling, and I get why you are upset. Let's talk about what is going on at lunch and figure out some things you could say or do when that happens."

For ages nine to twelve: "I hear you, and I believe you when you say it feels like everyone has it. Being the one who does not have the same thing as your friends is genuinely hard.

I want to work through this with you rather than just saying no and walking away."

Both scripts do the same thing up front: they name the emotion before they touch the rule. They treat the child as someone whose social world matters. And they open a conversation instead of slamming it shut. After that, you can move into your reasoning.

Next comes what family therapists often call values clarification. It works best when your child helps shape it instead of sitting through a lecture. Ask questions rather than making declarations. "What do you think our family cares about most when it comes to screens?" or "If you could make the rules, what would you keep and what would you change?" Kids can be surprisingly thoughtful when they feel consulted instead of cornered.

One mother, Priya, used what she called her "family filter" with her ten-year-old daughter. Whenever a new app, game, or device request came up, they ran it through three questions together: Does it match what we care about as a family? Is it right for your age? Can we set it up in a way that feels good for both of us? Sometimes the answer was yes. Her daughter got Minecraft after they talked it through and set up shared play sessions. Sometimes the answer was "not yet." And sometimes it was a clear no. Because the process stayed consistent and collaborative, her daughter stopped framing every request as a battle and started treating it like a negotiation.

Confidence in making different choices also comes from giving your child language they can actually use with peers. A nine-year-old who says, "My parents won't let me," puts all the weight on you and makes themselves sound powerless. A nine-year-old who says, "Yeah, I'm not really into that, but tell me about the part where you built the castle," keeps their footing and shifts the conversation. Practice these pivots at home the way you might practice what to do if a stranger offers something unsafe. Role-play is not silly. It is rehearsal. You can keep it light by turning it into a quick dinner game: take turns playing "the kid" and "the friend," and let your child practice until the words feel natural. Two or three rounds can be the difference between freezing and switching lanes smoothly.

Scripts your child can use with friends:

"I haven't played that one. What's it like?" (shows curiosity without committing)

"My family does screens differently, but it's cool. What else did you do this weekend?" (normalizes the difference and pivots)

"I'm more into [specific interest] right now." (positions the child as having their own preferences rather than being restricted)

The goal is a child who can hold a boundary without feeling embarrassed about it. Psychologists Edward Deci and Richard Ryan describe this as autonomous motivation: choosing a behavior because it fits your values, even when outside pressure pushes the other way. You do not get there with one perfect talk. You get there by consistently taking their social experience seriously, letting them in on the reasoning, and giving them words that help them stay part of the group without giving up their footing.

Understanding Gaming Giants and Social Currency

Three games dominate the social scene for the six-to-twelve age group right now: Roblox, Minecraft, and Fortnite. Each one works differently, carries different risks, and plays a different role in your child's social world. When you understand those differences, you have far more options than a blanket "no gaming" rule ever gives you.

Roblox is less a single game and more a platform containing millions of user-created games. Think of it as a huge digital playground where each area was built by a different person, with wildly uneven quality and content. A child might spend twenty minutes in a perfectly wholesome obstacle course, then wander into an experience with chat interactions that would make you uncomfortable. The social element is central to Roblox. Kids play together, chat, trade virtual items, and build shared worlds. For many children, saying "I play Roblox" is basically the same as saying, "I hang out at recess." It is a shared space where friendships form and get maintained.

Minecraft offers a more contained experience. In creative mode, it plays like digital LEGOs, with kids building structures, designing worlds, and experimenting with simple engineering ideas. Survival mode adds resource management and problem-solving. Minecraft can be played solo or in carefully controlled multiplayer settings. Of the three, it often offers the most room for creative, productive play and some of the easiest parental controls. Many families use it as a first game for exactly that reason (if I had to pick one starter game, Minecraft would be my choice, especially in creative mode on a shared device). Some educators have even brought Minecraft into classrooms for lessons on architecture, history, and basic circuitry, which hints at what it can be when it is used on purpose.

Fortnite is a battle royale game where up to one hundred players compete until one remains. The gameplay is fast, colorful, and built to be intensely stimulating. Its cultural footprint goes beyond the game through dances, character skins, and seasonal events that turn into school lunch conversation. Fortnite is rated T for Teen (ages thirteen and up), which gives you a clear external reference point when your under-thirteen child asks to play it.

One distinction that helps many parents is the difference between social gaming and solo gaming. Social gaming, where your child plays with friends, can support real connection. The Oxford Internet Institute has reported that people who play with friends often describe the experience as more socially satisfying than playing alone. Solo gaming, where a child disappears into a screen for long stretches with no real interaction, is more likely to slide into isolation and compulsive use.

That framing shifts the question. Instead of "Should my child play games?" you can ask, "How is my child playing, and who are they playing with?" A thirty-minute Minecraft session where your child and their best friend build a castle while talking is not the same thing as a two-hour solo Roblox session hopping through random experiences with strangers. When your family guidelines reflect that difference, kids tend to understand the reasoning more quickly. You are not saying "games are bad." You are saying, "Connection is welcome. Isolation is what worries me."

If you want to allow some gaming while keeping boundaries, age-appropriate alternatives matter. Kids ages six to eight often do best with games that have limited or no online interaction: Minecraft in creative mode on a family device, LEGO-based games, or coding games like ScratchJr. Kids ages nine to twelve can handle more social gaming when guardrails are in place: approved friend lists, clear time limits, and the device in a shared family space where you can hear the conversations.

One father, David, handled his eleven-year-old's Fortnite request by watching gameplay videos together and talking about what they noticed. His son saw the violence and the intensity and admitted it was "kind of a lot." They agreed to revisit it at thirteen. In the meantime, his son started a Minecraft server with three close friends. Six months later, he told David the Minecraft server was actually more fun because they could build things that lasted instead of wiping everything out each round.

Financial Digital Literacy and Microtransactions

If gaming culture is the social pressure your child feels at school, microtransactions are the financial pressure waiting inside the game. Most kids between six and twelve have almost no real grasp of how digital money works, which is exactly why the model works so well.

Robux (the currency in Roblox), V-Bucks (Fortnite's currency), and Minecoins (Minecraft's marketplace currency) all work the same way. Real money gets converted into a virtual currency with an intentionally confusing exchange rate. One thousand Robux costs roughly $12.50, but a child does not think, "I am spending twelve dollars on a virtual hat." They think, "It only costs 400 Robux." That abstraction is the point. When money stops looking like money, spending it feels painless. Adults fall for the same dynamic with casino chips and tap-to-pay; kids are even more vulnerable because the part of the brain responsible for impulse control is still under construction.

This is also a clean opening to teach financial literacy that will matter long after Roblox is old news. The idea is simple: digital money is real money in a costume.

For ages six to eight: Use physical money as a bridge. Put ten dollars in coins on the table and say: "This is how much that Robux package costs. If you held this money in your hand, would you trade all of it for a character outfit that you can only see on a screen?" When young kids can see and touch the money, their decisions usually get more careful. Some families use a "digital spending jar" where the child has to physically move real coins out of a jar before any digital purchase is approved. The cost becomes tangible every time.

For ages nine to twelve: You can go deeper into the business model. Explain that many game companies make more money from virtual items than from selling the game itself. Fortnite is free to download because its revenue depends on microtransactions. Ask your child: "If the game is free, how does the company make billions of dollars?" Let them work it out. Once a kid understands the incentives, the spell breaks a little.

Preventing surprise charges takes practical systems, not just good talks. A family in Seattle discovered a $340 credit card charge after their seven-year-old made repeated small purchases in Roblox over two weeks, each one under five dollars. The child had no concept of the accumulating total. To prevent this scenario:

Remove stored payment methods from any device your child uses. If a purchase requires physically entering a credit card number each time, impulse buying drops dramatically. On Apple devices, enable "Ask to Buy" through Family Sharing. On Android, require authentication for every Google Play purchase. On gaming consoles, set up parental controls that require a PIN for any transaction.

Establish a digital spending allowance if you choose to allow purchases at all. A fixed monthly amount (perhaps three to five dollars) that the child manages themselves teaches budgeting in a low-stakes way. When the money is gone, it is gone until next month. That creates real trade-offs. Do they want the character skin now, or do they want to wait and save for a bigger item? Those small choices are practice for later.

Several families also like a "cooling off" rule: when your child wants to buy something, they write it down and wait forty-eight hours. If they still want it after two days, and it fits within their allowance, they can buy it. Behavioral economist Dan Ariely has written extensively about how adding even small amounts of friction reduces impulse purchases. You will probably find your child forgets about a lot of the items on their wish list before the forty-eight hours are up.

None of this is only about gaming. Your child is growing up in a world of subscriptions, in-app purchases, limited-time offers, and one-click buying. Teaching them to pause and do a quick reality check is a skill they will use constantly.

Delaying Social Media: The Age 13 Conversation

If your child is between six and twelve, social media can feel like a future problem. The pressure shows up earlier than most parents expect, though, and having a clear framework now keeps you from making reactive decisions later.

The legal starting point is straightforward. The Children's Online Privacy Protection Act, known as COPPA, is a federal law that prohibits online platforms from collecting personal data from children under thirteen without verified parental consent. That is why most social media platforms, including Instagram, TikTok, Snapchat, and Facebook, set their minimum age at thirteen. It is compliance.

Explaining that gives you an external anchor and takes some heat out of the "my parents are being unfair" dynamic. Here is how to frame it at different ages:

For ages six to eight: "There is a rule that says kids under thirteen are not old enough for those apps yet. It is like how you have to be a certain height to ride some roller coasters. It is about being ready, and you are not quite there yet."

For ages nine to twelve: "There is actually a law called COPPA that says companies are not allowed to collect information from kids under thirteen. That is why these apps say you have to be thirteen to sign up. Some kids lie about their age to get around it, but that creates real problems, and our family follows the rules even when other families make different choices."

The nine-to-twelve conversation often gets more pushback because kids this age notice that some classmates already have accounts. This is where your boundary-holding scripts matter.

When your child says: "But my friends all have Instagram."
You can respond: "I know some of your friends have accounts, and I understand that makes you feel like you are

missing out. Our family's decision is based on the law and on what we believe is best for you right now. That does not mean we will never talk about it again. When you turn thirteen, we will revisit this together and figure out what makes sense."

When your child says: "You just don't trust me."
You can respond: "I trust you a lot, actually. This is about the platforms themselves. These apps are built by teams whose job is to keep people scrolling as long as possible. I would not hand you the keys to a car before you learned to drive, and I feel the same way about social media. We are going to prepare for it together so that when you do start, you are ready."

When your child says: "I'll just use a friend's account."
You can respond: "I appreciate you being honest about that possibility. Here is what I need you to understand: if something goes wrong on someone else's account, whether it is a message from a stranger or content that upsets you, it becomes much harder for me to help you. Having your own account when you are old enough means we can set it up with the right protections together."

These talks go better when they are ongoing rather than a single sit-down speech. Families who handle the transition smoothly usually start discussing it years before it happens. Between ages nine and twelve, you can begin prepping your child by talking about what social media is, how it makes money, and what skills they will need before they use it.

Think of this preparation as a "digital learner's permit." Before a teenager gets a driver's license, they learn the rules, practice with supervision, and earn more independence over time. You can borrow that model. Between ages ten and twelve, introduce concepts like how algorithms decide what to show you, why "likes" and "followers" mess with social comparison, what a digital footprint is, and how to spot manipulative or misleading content. These concepts were covered in the previous chapter on digital literacy, and they form a foundation for later. You might dedicate one family conversation per month to a single topic: one month you talk about recommendation algorithms, the next month you look at what happens to a photo once it is posted. Small lessons add up.

Some families create a list of milestones their child needs to show before social media access at thirteen is even on the table. These might include: consistently following existing screen time agreements, showing the ability to evaluate online content critically, handling negative feedback without spiraling, and understanding privacy settings and why they matter. When the criteria are clear and discussed in advance, the thirteenth birthday is not an automatic green light. It is just a checkpoint.

One message worth repeating in the pre-teen years is that delaying social media is about timing, not punishment. The American Psychological Association's 2023 health advisory on social media use in adolescence points to the way heavy use can amplify sleep problems and social comparison, especially for vulnerable kids. Your child probably will not care about a health advisory. But they can understand this: "We want you to have more time to figure out who you are before you step into a space that is very good at pulling you into everyone else's opinions."

Marcus, the father from the opening of this chapter, eventually found a rhythm with these conversations. His son still complained sometimes about gaming restrictions and the social media delay. Over time, though, the tone changed from "You're ruining my life" to "I get why, but I still wish I could." That shift did not make the problem disappear, but it made it workable. It meant the conversation stayed open, which is usually the only real win you need.

Your Action Steps:

- Practice the validation-first response this week. The next time your child says "everyone else has it," start with "I hear you, and that sounds hard" before you move into reasoning or boundary-setting.
- Research the specific games your child is asking about or already playing. Spend fifteen minutes watching

gameplay footage of Roblox, Minecraft, or Fortnite so you can have informed conversations rather than reactive ones.

- Audit your family's payment settings on every device your child uses. Remove stored credit cards, enable purchase authentication, and consider a small digital spending allowance with a clear monthly cap.
- Have an age-appropriate COPPA conversation with your child this week using the scripts provided, and establish your family's position on social media before the pressure intensifies.
- Create your family's "digital learner's permit" checklist: write down three to five specific skills or behaviors your child needs to demonstrate before social media access becomes a conversation at age thirteen.

CHAPTER 10

Troubleshooting Common Challenges: Quick Solutions for Tough Situations

Sophia found the tablet under her daughter's pillow at 10:47 p.m. on a Tuesday. The screen was still warm. Her eight-year-old, Mia, had been watching YouTube videos for at least an hour after lights out, using a device Sophia thought was locked in the kitchen drawer. Mia had figured out the drawer's childproof latch three weeks earlier and had been sneaking the tablet to bed every night since. Sophia's first instinct was anger. Her second was confusion. They had rules. They had conversations. They had a family media agreement pinned to the refrigerator. How did they end up here?

If you have kids between six and twelve, you'll run into some version of this. The strategies and systems from earlier chapters work, and they work well. But day-to-day life rarely follows the plan. Siblings fight over whose turn it is. Grandparents hand over iPads to keep the peace during visits. A kid who followed the rules for months suddenly backslides. It can feel like you blew it. More often, it's a moment where you get to tighten the system and teach a skill that actually sticks.

Think of this chapter as a practical guide for those moments. Each section tackles a common challenge with concrete scripts, age-appropriate strategies, and step-by-step fixes you can use the day the problem shows up.

The Sneaky Device Use Problem

Sneaky device use hits a nerve because it feels personal. You set a boundary, and your child worked around it. That discovery can spark frustration, disappointment, and worry all at once, which is exactly when parents tend to go too big. Before you respond, pause and zoom out.

Kids between six and twelve are built to test limits. Sneaking a device after bedtime or during homework has the same root as sneaking a cookie before dinner. The thing is tempting, and impulse control is still developing at this age. That context does not excuse the behavior. It does change the story from "my child is lying to me" to "my child is struggling to manage something that pulls hard."

Prevention over punishment. Your most effective move is usually to make it harder to repeat. If your child smuggled a tablet to bed, the device now sleeps somewhere else: a locked cabinet, your bedroom closet, or a charging station outside their room. If they accessed a phone during homework, the phone stays with you until homework is checked and finished. These are environmental changes, the same idea as not buying the junk food in the first place instead of asking everyone to "just use willpower." You adjust the environment to support the behavior you want, rather than expecting a developing brain to resist temptation every night.

For children ages six to eight, keep the conversation brief, warm, and focused on the reason behind the rule:

"I found the tablet under your pillow. I know those videos are really fun to watch. The reason we stop screens before bed is that the bright light makes it harder for your brain to fall asleep, and your brain needs sleep to grow. The tablet is going to stay in my room at night from now on. That will make bedtime easier."

The structure matters. You name what happened, you acknowledge the pull, you restate the reason for the boundary, and then you make a practical change. No shaming. No drawn-out lecture. No consequences that have nothing to do with screens.

For children ages nine to twelve, you can add more accountability and a clear path back to trust:

"I found the tablet in your room after lights out. I'm disappointed because we agreed on when screens end for the night, and sneaking it breaks that agreement. I get that it's hard to stop when something is interesting. Here's what's going to happen: the tablet stays in the kitchen every night,

and in two weeks we'll talk about whether you've shown me you can stick to our agreements in other areas too. If that goes well, we can revisit how this works."

That two-week "trust rebuild" window is useful at this age. Nine- to twelve-year-olds care more about autonomy than they did a few years ago. A specific way to earn back privileges gives them something concrete to work toward, instead of leaving them stuck in "I'm grounded forever" thinking.

What to avoid. Fight the urge to stack punishments. Taking away the device, canceling a playdate, and adding extra chores in one burst of frustration tells your child you are reacting, not leading. One clear, logical consequence tied directly to the behavior beats three unrelated ones.

Skip the surveillance spiral, too. Installing tracking software on every device, reading every message, and checking browser history hourly might feel responsible. For many kids in this age range, it lands as "They don't trust me," and it can push the behavior further underground. Save intensive monitoring for real safety concerns, like contact with strangers or repeated exposure to harmful content. For everyday rule-breaking, lean on environmental controls and a straightforward conversation.

If sneaky device use keeps happening even after you change the setup, treat that as a clue. Is your child using the device to cope with anxiety or social stress? Are they hooked on content that is designed to keep them clicking, like games built around intermittent rewards? That pattern calls for calm curiosity: *"I've noticed this keeps happening even after we changed where the tablet lives. Help me understand what's going on. Is there something about bedtime that feels hard right now?"* Sometimes the device is not the main issue. It is just the most visible one.

Sibling Digital Conflicts

If you have more than one child, you have heard "That's not fair!" recently, probably at full volume. Digital conflicts between siblings usually fall into three categories: arguments about total screen time, fights over shared devices, and complaints about different rules for different ages. Each one has a fix.

Fair versus equal. The most common complaint is that one child gets more screen time or different privileges than another. A nine-year-old watches her twelve-year-old brother play a game she is restricted from, and the protest starts. The urge to make every rule identical feels clean and "fair." It usually backfires. A six-year-old and an eleven-year-old have different attention spans, different homework demands, and different social lives. Treating them the same ignores those realities.

The language that tends to work is simple: "Fair means getting what you need. Equal means getting the same thing." Use it often enough that it becomes part of the family script. You can introduce it like this:

"Your brother has different screen time because he's older and his brain handles it differently. When you're his age, your screen time will grow too. Fair means everyone gets what works for their age."

With younger kids, ages six to eight, make it even more concrete: *"You get to stay up until 8:00, and your brother stays up until 9:00. It's the same idea. Older kids get a later bedtime and a little more screen time."* Bedtime is a difference most kids already accept, so it helps the screen time difference make sense.

Age-gap challenges. When siblings span the six-to-twelve range, the older child's content will drift into the younger child's world. A ten-year-old playing Fortnite in the living room means the seven-year-old is absorbing it as a spectator, even without a controller. Two moves help.

Start with screen zones. The older child's gaming happens in a specific room, ideally one with a door, during times when the younger child is busy elsewhere. This is a logistics fix, and logistics tend to beat rules that require a seven-year-old to "just stop watching" an action-filled screen.

Then give the younger child a real alternative during the older child's screen time. "Your brother is going to play his game for thirty minutes. During that time, you and I are going to build that Lego set together." You are not asking the younger child to tolerate exclusion with nothing to do. You are filling the gap with something that can actually compete.

Shared device protocols. When siblings share a tablet or computer, scheduling prevents most conflicts. A written schedule posted where both children can see it, with specific blocks and clear handoff times, keeps you out of the referee role.

A practical protocol looks like this: Child A uses the device from 4:00 to 4:30. At 4:30, a timer goes off, and Child A saves their work or game progress and hands the device to Child B. If Child A refuses to hand it over, Child A loses their slot the following day. If Child B interrupts Child A's turn, Child B's turn starts five minutes late. The consequences are predictable, proportional, and explained ahead of time.

For families with three or more children sharing devices, a rotating priority system works well. Each child gets "first pick" on a rotating day. Monday is Ella's day to choose first, Tuesday is Marco's, Wednesday is Lily's. It cuts out the daily negotiation and gives each child a reliable sense of control.

One often-missed fix is separate user profiles. Most tablets and computers allow multiple accounts. Each child gets their own login with age-appropriate apps, saved progress, and content restrictions. That alone can prevent the "someone messed up my game" fight and stop younger kids from wandering into older content by accident.

When Parents and Grandparents Disagree

You spend weeks building a screen-time structure at home. Then the kids visit Grandma and come back having watched four hours of cartoons, played unlimited games on Grandpa's phone, and eaten ice cream for dinner. It can feel like your system got wiped out in a weekend by the people who raised you.

Disagreements between parents and grandparents about technology are common and awkward because you are managing two relationships at once: your relationship with your child and your relationship with your own parents or in-laws. The goal is not to "win." It is to get enough consistency that your rules still mean something. That usually takes a specific order of conversations.

Start with a private conversation. The worst time to address screen disagreements is in front of your children. Kids notice cracks fast, and watching adults argue about rules teaches them that rules depend on which adult they ask. Talk when the children are asleep, at school, or otherwise out of earshot.

Lead with respect and shared goals. Grandparents who allow lots of screens are rarely trying to undermine you. Usually they want to be the "fun" adult, they want visits to go smoothly, or they truly think you are being too strict. Appreciation lands better than criticism, and it keeps the conversation from turning into a power struggle.

Try this: *"Mom, the kids love visiting you, and I love that you want them to have a great time. I want to talk about screens because we've been working on something at home, and it would help a lot if we were on the same page."*

From there, get specific about what you are asking. Vague requests like "limit their screen time" leave too much room for interpretation. Offer a simple framework instead: *"We'd love it if screen time at your house stayed under an hour per visit. After that, the kids would probably love doing puzzles with you, or baking, or working in the garden. They talk about your garden all the time."*

That last part is not fluff. It gives the grandparent a role that no device can replace. Baking together, card games, the garden, a walk around the block, a small "project" that lives at Grandma's house: those are the anchors that make visits feel special, and they also make it easier to say no to another episode.

Compromise techniques. If a grandparent pushes back, you may need a middle ground rather than a carbon copy of your home rules. A workable compromise might be: screens are allowed, but only pre-approved content, and meals and bedtime stay aligned with home routines. A little extra flexibility at Grandma's is fine. What matters is that the big boundaries hold, especially around bedtime, age-appropriate content, and overall balance.

If a grandparent resists strongly, framing the request around the child's specific needs can land better than explaining your whole philosophy. *"Mia has been having trouble sleeping after long screen sessions, and her pediatrician mentioned keeping screens limited before bed. Could we make sure the tablet goes off by 6:00 when she's at your house?"* This sidesteps the "you're telling me how to grandparent" dynamic and keeps the focus on the child.

When the disagreement is between co-parents. Everything above matters even more when two parents in the same household disagree about tech rules. If Mom says yes and Dad says no, kids will test that fault line until it becomes the main event. Commit to one rule: present a unified answer to the children, then debate it privately. The phrase *"Let me talk to your mom/dad and we'll get back to you"* is one of the most useful sentences you can practice. It buys time, prevents mixed messages, and keeps the decision-making between adults.

Recovering from Setbacks and Mistakes

Three months into your family's screen-time plan, everything slides. A rainy holiday week turns into a free-for-all. A brutal stretch at work means you hand over the tablet more often than you intended, just to get through dinner or one last email. Then your child, who had been doing fine with the boundaries, starts pushing back with the intensity you remember from week one. This is a setback. It is also normal.

Normal regression patterns. Kids between six and twelve tend to regress during predictable windows: school transitions, family disruptions like a move or a new sibling, illness, holidays, and the start of summer break. Routine loosens, stress runs higher, and screens feel extra comforting. If you expect some wobble during these seasons, you are less likely to panic when it shows up.

Parents regress, too. A week of poor sleep, a demanding work project, or conflict at home drains the energy it takes to enforce limits. You reach for the easy button because you are tired. That is not a character flaw. It is a systems problem: the plan did not match the week you were having.

Getting back on track. The biggest mistake after a setback is trying to snap back overnight. "Starting tomorrow, we're back to all the rules, no exceptions." From your child's point of view, they just lived through a week or two of expanded access. A sudden clampdown feels like punishment, and it often triggers a power struggle.

A graduated return usually works better. If your normal limit is one hour a day and the past two weeks averaged three hours, step down over four to five days:

Day one: two and a half hours. Day two: two hours. Day three: one and a half hours. Day four: back to one hour.

Explain it in plain language: *"We got off track with screens over the break. This week we're going to step back down to our normal schedule. Today you get two and a half hours, and we'll reduce a little each day until we're back to our usual routine by Thursday."*

Two things make this work. First, it gives your child's brain time to adjust to lower stimulation. Second, it feels predictable. Predictable beats punitive.

Learning from failures. Every setback leaves a paper trail. Once things calm down, take ten minutes and look at what happened. Ask yourself three questions:

What triggered the regression? Was it a specific event, a change in routine, or a gradual drift?

Which part of the system broke first? Did the environmental controls fail, did the schedule collapse, or did you and your co-parent stop enforcing consistently?

What one change would make the system more resilient? Maybe you need a "vacation rules" protocol that allows slightly more screen time during holidays but still keeps a cap. Maybe the after-school transition plan needs a backup for rainy days. Maybe you need a quick check-in with your co-parent every Sunday evening to stay aligned for the week ahead.

Treat setbacks as information and you can adjust without turning it into a family crisis. If I had to pick one habit that prevents repeat setbacks, it is putting the friction in the right place: make screens easy to start when they are allowed, and mildly annoying to access when they are not (a consistent charging spot outside bedrooms does a lot of quiet work).

If you recognize your family in several of these scenarios, you do not need a brand-new philosophy. You need one or two practical tweaks and a little follow-through. Pick the problem that is causing the most friction this week and tighten that first.

Your Action Steps:

- If sneaky device use has been an issue, make one environmental change today: move the device to a new overnight location, enable scheduled downtime, or switch to a charging station outside your child's bedroom.

- Create a shared device schedule for siblings this week with written time blocks and clear handoff rules, and post it where everyone can see it.
- Have a private, respectful conversation with any grandparent or co-parent who is inconsistent with your screen time structure. Use the scripts provided, and focus on one or two concrete requests rather than trying to rewrite everything at once.
- If your family is currently in a setback period, map out a four-to-five-day graduated return to your normal screen time limits starting tomorrow. Tell your child the plan in advance so it feels predictable rather than like a surprise punishment.
- Spend ten minutes this weekend reflecting on your most recent screen time challenge. Identify the trigger, the first failure point in the system, and one specific adjustment that would strengthen your approach going forward.

Conclusion

You picked up this guide because something felt off. Maybe it was the glazed look in your child's eyes after too long on a tablet. Maybe it was the meltdown that followed when you said, "Time's up." Or maybe it was the quieter worry that shows up in the middle of a work meeting: *Am I getting this right? Is my kid going to be okay?*

Yes. Your kid is going to be okay. And if you made it this far, you are paying attention in a way that already puts you ahead of the drift.

Be honest about what you have actually done here. You now understand how the developing brain responds to screens, why dopamine loops pull kids back to certain apps, and what executive function looks like at six versus twelve. You have language for the problem that goes beyond guilt and guesswork. It is hard to change what you cannot name.

Better yet, you have systems. Not vague intentions. Not a list of things to feel bad about. Real structures: a family media agreement with your child's input baked in, charging stations outside bedrooms, and scheduled downtime that your devices enforce even when your willpower is running low at 8 p.m. on a Wednesday. You have scripts for the conversations that used to end in tears or slammed doors. You have transition rituals that move your child from screen to non-screen activities without a fight every single time.

You also have something less measurable, but just as useful: a shift in perspective. Screens are not the enemy. Technology is the water your children will swim in for the rest of their lives. Your job was never to drain the pool. It was to teach them to swim, and to recognize a riptide when they feel one pulling. The difference between a child who is consumed by tech and a child who can use it without getting used by it usually comes down to guardrails, conversations, and the example they live with between ages six and twelve. That window is open right now.

Some of what you learned will click immediately. Environmental changes can move the needle fast: shifting a tablet to a common area, setting up a router schedule, or putting a visible daily routine chart where everyone can see it. (In my experience, the charging station outside bedrooms is one of the quickest wins.) Other pieces take time. Teaching your nine-year-old to notice when a game is built to keep them playing past the point of enjoyment develops over months of small conversations, not one big lecture. And tightening up your own screen habits into something you would actually want your child to copy takes patience, too.

You will have setbacks. Holidays will blow up your schedule. A new game will rip through the fourth grade like wildfire, and your child will suddenly want it more than oxygen. A co-parent or grandparent will hand over an unsupervised iPad at the worst possible moment. When that happens, go back to basics. Identify the trigger. Find the first failure point in your system. Make one adjustment. Step back down gradually. Talk about it without turning it into a character flaw.

The families who do well with this are not the ones who get it perfect. They are the ones who recover quickly. Think of it as operational resilience. Your system does not need to be unbreakable. It needs to be easy to repair.

One more thing to keep in mind. Every conversation you have with your child about why a certain app wants their attention, every time you sit next to them, watch what they are watching, and ask real questions about it, you are making a deposit. Not into an account with a visible balance, but into trust and judgment that build over years. You are creating a relationship where your child will tell you when something online feels weird. You are strengthening the kind of critical thinking they will need at fifteen, when you are no longer hovering nearby. You are helping them practice focus, patience, and the skill of moving through boredom instead of reflexively fleeing it.

That is not small.

Now pick one thing. Not five. One. Look at your family's biggest friction point with screens this week and use the strategy that fits. Put the system in place. Have the conversation. Move the charging cable. Do it today, while it is still specific and real, not an abstract plan you keep postponing.

Your children are watching, and not just what is on the screen. They are watching how you set limits, how you recover when you slip, and how you decide what gets your attention.

Start there. Adjust as you go.

Sources

CHAPTER 2: UNDERSTANDING YOUR CHILD'S DIGITAL BRAIN: WHY KIDS GET 'HOOKED' AND HOW TO BREAK THE CYCLE

(2017-06-28). *ncbi.nlm.nih.gov*. https://www.ncbi.nlm.nih.gov/pmc/articles/PMC5492743/

(2024-01-16). *Don't Let Screen Time Interfere With Self Regulation for Kids*. https://www.komusodesign.com/blogs/stories/dont-let-screen-time-interfere-with-self-regulation-for-kids

(2022). *How to Get Healthier Dopamine Highs - TIME*. https://time.com/6155109/healthier-dopamine-highs/

(2021-09). *Does a Young Child Have Temporal Awareness? - Psychology Today*. https://www.psychologytoday.com/us/blog/the-speed-of-life/202109/does-a-young-child-have-temporal-awareness

(2016). *Time Perception Mechanisms at Central Nervous System - PMC - NIH*. https://pmc.ncbi.nlm.nih.gov/articles/PMC4830363/

(2019-07-17). *nngroup.com*. https://www.nngroup.com/articles/red-not-best-choice-urgent-notifications/

(2024). *Building Self-Regulation in Childhood with Neuroscience - Medbridge*. https://www.medbridge.com/blog/self-regulation-in-childhood

(2011). *Dopamine in motivational control: rewarding, aversive, and alerting*. https://pmc.ncbi.nlm.nih.gov/articles/PMC3032992/

(2012). *Children and time | BPS - British Psychological Society*. https://www.bps.org.uk/psychologist/children-and-time

(2018-01-02). *theguardian.com*. https://www.theguardian.com/technology/2018/jan/02/attention-economy-ux-tristan-harris

CHAPTER 5: THE POST-SCREEN MELTDOWN MAP: SMOOTH TRANSITIONS EVERY TIME

(2021). *What Does Too Much Screen Time Do to Children's Brains?*.

https://healthmatters.nyp.org/what-does-too-much-screen-time-do-to-childrens-brains/

(2023). *The effects of screen time on children: The latest research parents* .... https://health.choc.org/the-effects-of-screen-time-on-children-the-latest-research-parents-should-know/

(2014-08). *Internet Guidance on Time Out: Inaccuracies, Omissions, and What* https://pmc.ncbi.nlm.nih.gov/articles/PMC4179870/

(2024). *A scoping review of the impact of screen time on cognitive function* https://pubmed.ncbi.nlm.nih.gov/40656848/

(2023-08-01). *Back to School: How Screen Time Affects Children's Brains.* https://www.cedars-sinai.org/newsroom/back-to-school-how-screen-time-affects-childrens-developing-brains/

(2023-05-15). *Stanford-led study highlights the importance of letting kids take the* .... https://ed.stanford.edu/news/stanford-led-study-highlights-importance-letting-kids-take-lead

(2024). *Neurodivergent Kids and Screen Time - Child Mind Institute.* https://childmind.org/article/screens-and-neurodivergent-kids/

(2023). *Early Childhood Brain Development: The Key to Building Executive* .... https://reflectionsciences.com/early-childhood-brain-development-the-key-to-building-executive-function-skills/

(2014). *The Effects of Screens on Kids and How to Set Limits.* https://www.findapsychologist.org/the-effects-of-screens-on-kids-and-how-to-set-limits-exploring-the-cognitive-psychosocial-and-psychological-impact/

(2025-06). *Screen time and emotional problems in kids: A vicious circle?.* https://www.apa.org/news/press/releases/2025/06/screen-time-problems-children

Made in the USA
Monee, IL
03 October 2026

64834643R10095